BOOBS AND BISCUITS

Four Generations of Southern Family Recipes

Printing by Falcon Press LLC, Nashville, Tennessee.

Editing and layout assistance by David Owen.

Printed and bound in the United States of America.

TABLE OF CONTENTS

A note on the cover:

I was given the moniker "Butter" by my friend "Koops" for hogging all the butter during our neighborhood cooking classes. She would show up, grab the butter bell and tell me to "keep my distance" until everyone had had their fill. There is something special in that fun relationship, so I have embraced her calling me "Butter" fully and I return the greeting with "Hey there Koops".

I believe absolutely that *everything* is better with a fabulous butter!!

WHY A COOKBOOK?

To start, I believe that the title might need a little explanation. I met my husband when he was twelve and I was fourteen. It was my "assets" that caught his eye but it was feeding him (particularly biscuits) that got him hooked and landed. I learned what he liked and I made sure to keep him in food heaven and I used family recipes (from both sides) in the preparation of these dishes. Even now 43 years later, doing this for my family fills my heart and their tummies and the eating of those dishes makes them feel cared for in a way that nothing else can. I cook because I care that they feel full, happy, and cared for!

As many are aware, food is central to southern culture. There is not an event you can name that we do not deem food worthy. A baby is born ... bring that momma a casserole. It's a sporting event ... break out the grill. Family reunion (yes we still do these) ... bust out your BEST dessert. Holidays? Oh, come on y'all!

Preserving these recipes for my daughter and the generations to come was important to me. Instead of stacks of cookbooks (many falling apart) and piles of fading pieces of paper, we now have a central repository for the recipes and associated memories in this cookbook. So, this collection of recipes comes from four generations of my family, the church and school fundraising cookbooks we collected, handwritten recipes from friends, our own personal favorites and the random unidentified recipe found tucked away in a book.

This book is called "Boobs and Biscuits" because I caught my man's attention with one and kept him happy with the other. Even now (43 years later), when asked what he loves most about me, his favorite thing to say is...

...well, you know.

DEDICATION

A very important part of my choosing to release this cookbook commercially is that it provides me with yet another way to care for those I love. The decision had been made to publish prior to the emergence of COVID-19, but the impact of this virus on those I care about added a sense of urgency to completing the cookbook. So, we ask your forgiveness in advance if things are less than perfect. We gave it our sleep-deprived best effort.

A portion of the net proceeds from the sale of this cookbook will supplement the income of the elderly members of my family, help support the family farms, and provide additional income for my Falcon Press staff, the family of my heart, who worked with me to develop and produce this book.

This book is dedicated to my husband, my brother, the many women (named and unnamed) who contributed to my rearing and this cookbook, and to those in my Falcon Press family who were willing to stand beside me when times got tough.

Much love and respect to (in no particular order as we all know how Southerners are about precedent):

GG, Grandma Gayle, Keeley, Kathy, Aunt Biba, Aunt Mackie, Aunt Tillie, Aunt Ann, Nana, Momma Dot, Aunt Gayle, my tribe of adopted children (Tara, Candy, Kendra, Michelle, Virginia, Stephanie, Pritch, Alex, Zoe etc.), my Falcon Press staff and family, my brother (who thought this a brilliant idea) and, of course, my husband Toby who persistently and kindly kept encouraging me to FINISH THE DAMN BOOK.

DISCLAIMER

I am not a Chef. I am a rural kitchen cook (with the power of a Chef in MY kitchen). Recipes for me are considered guidelines and I color outside the lines quite a lot. I cook by taste, touch and smell. Using recipes as a road map, I experiment as I go along, adding things that I think make it better and taking out things (judiciously) that I do not like. You should evaluate each recipe included here to determine how you can better it to your tastes and needs. There are no absolutes! Where I have not provided measurements, you should add and taste, add and taste, add and taste until you are happy. Be adventurous!

Enjoy!

IMPORTANT NOTE: If you do not eat butter or bacon grease, 1) you don't know what you are missing, and 2) this cookbook will be an adventure.

ESSENTIAL TOOLS IN A COUNTRY KITCHEN

Great tools can make cooking MUCH easier and can help you more easily achieve the results desired. However, there are always workarounds and handy "Grandma Gayle" suggestions are noted where applicable. Here are the tools that I find invaluable.

- Cast Iron Skillet (at the very least a medium sized one)
- Dutch Oven
- Non-Stick Skillets with Lids
- Pots (at least one large soup pot and one small pot with a pouring edge) with Lids and a Double Boiler (or just two pans that fit together as needed)
- Whisk (or a fork and a strong wrist)
- Pastry Blender / Cutter (or two butter knives)
- Pastry Mat (or a clean kitchen counter)
- Chopper / Scooper (or a paper plate edge or spatula)
- Pie Plate and Loaf Pan
- Colander (or just the lid of the pot)
- Biscuit Cutter (or a small glass with a neat edge)
- Baking Dishes
- Mixing Bowls (or any bowl according to Grandma Gayle)
- Chopping Board
- SHARP Knives
- Turning and Mixing Spatulas
- Measuring Cups and Spoons
- Tongs
- Ladle (or a coffee cup)
- Peeler (or a paring knife)
- Rolling Pin (both for cooking and disciplining)
- Electric Hand Mixer
- Oven Mitts (or kitchen hand towels, shop rags or your husband)

ESSENTIAL INGREDIENTS IN A COUNTRY KITCHEN

C'mon y'all. These are just the things any self respecting Southerner has in their kitchen.

- Butter (LOTS of it!) Both Salted and Unsalted
- Bacon Grease
  (Yep. Keep that grease in an airtight container in your fridge. You are gonna want that. Trust me on this.)
- Salt
- Pepper
- Fresh Produce (MOSTLY :)
- All-Purpose Flour (I NEVER use Self-Rising Flour)
- Baking Powder
- Baking Soda (Cooks and Cleans)
- Sugar (the real stuff)
- Milk (NOT Skim ... that is NOT Milk)
- Bacon (this is not just for breakfast)
- Olive Oil (a more recent addition and a nod at an attempt to make things a little healthier)

MY FAVORITE THINGS

- THE OTHER TWO PEOPLE IN MY PARTY OF THREE
- Wright's Bacon
- Quaker Oatmeal
- Land O Lakes BUTTER
- Fresh Eggs from my Sister (Oaklea Farm)
- Gold Medal All Purpose Flour
- Maldon Finishing Salt
- Clabber Girl Baking Powder
- FairLife Milk
- Beautiful Granny Smith Apples
- Ceylon Cinnamon
- Nielsen Massey Madagascar Vanilla
- Blue Oven Fresh Bread
- Equator Coffee
- Better Than Bouillon
- Rookwood Pottery
- Blackberry Farm Blackberry Jam

Breakfast
(all day)

IT ALL STARTED WITH BISCUITS

It goes without saying that the biscuits started it all. Here's the recipe that my husband loves! Please feel free to modify it to make it your own!

❖ Ingredients:

- All-Purpose Flour - 2 cups sifted plus extra for kneading
- Salt - 1 tsp
- Baking Powder - 4 tsp
- Sugar - 1 tbl
- Unsalted Butter (COLD) - 1 Stick (8 tbl)
- Milk - 3/4-1 cup

❖ Tools:

- Pastry Cutter (or 2 butter knives)
- Measuring Cup and Measuring Spoons
- Spatula
- Large Bowl
- Cookie Sheet
- Biscuit Cutter (or a small glass with a neat edge)
- Parchment Paper (or not)

❖ Directions:

- Preheat oven to 425 degrees.
- Cover cookie sheet with parchment paper.
- Mix flour, sugar, salt and baking powder in a large bowl.
- Cut cold butter into small pieces and add to dry mix.
- Using a pastry cutter (or two butter knives) cut the butter into the dry mix until it is the size of small peas.
- Add milk a little at a time and mix after each addition until you have a slightly wet dough.
- Turn the dough out onto a dry, clean and floured surface.
- Sprinkle a little flour on top to make it easier to handle and then begin to gently knead and fold the dough. Careful here. Not too much kneading ... handle gently.
- After folding and kneading between 5 and 10 folds, pat to desired thickness (I generally aim for about 1") and cut with a biscuit cutter.
- Place on the cookie sheet about 1" apart and bake until the desired color is achieved.

Note: Do not put in an oven that has not been fully preheated. Those crunchy brown bottoms are a favorite for very few. Also, make a big batch and freeze the ones you do not need, saving them for another day.

Reynolds KITCHEN

OTHER USES FOR BISCUIT DOUGH

You can do a lot of things with biscuit dough. It can be made savory with the addition of cheese, herbs and sausage (or a combination thereof) or slightly modified and dropped in a soup to make dumplings. It can be transformed into scones or shortcake. The dough can be rolled out and ingredients rolled into it to become most anything you would like from sausage pinwheels to a spin on cinnamon rolls. I encourage you to experiment with whatever you have in your refrigerator and cabinets to create your own recipes. The most satisfying foods are the ones that resonate with us. Follow your heart. What follows here are some of the variations that I have found work for my family and myself. Enjoy!

- Cheddar biscuits can be made by the addition of finely shredded cheddar cheese to the dry mix prior to the addition of the milk. You will skip the kneading and folding and just use a tablespoon to scoop spoonfuls onto the cookie sheet. Reduce your oven temperature to 375 degrees and watch them closely until they reach your desired level of "doneness". These are awesome with a bowl of potato soup!
- Cinnamon Rolled Biscuits can be created by rolling out biscuit dough on a floured surface to a 1/4" rectangle, generously coating the dough with a layer of soft butter and sprinkling it with cinnamon sugar prior to rolling it up from long side to long side. Seal the edge and use a wet, sharp knife to cut 1" slices. Place in a buttered baking dish with sides touching and bake at 375 degrees for approximately 15-20 minutes. Cool and then lightly pour over your homemade icing (confectioner sugar, cinnamon, a little milk or cream, a dash of vanilla flavoring and a little softened butter).
- Drop Dumplings are made by simply dropping spoonfuls of modified biscuit dough into very hot broth and covering to cook until they are fluffy (6-8 minutes). See page 40.
- Sausage Pinwheels - See page 12.
- Sausage Balls - See page 13.
- Blueberry Scones - See page 14.
- Spiced Pumpkin Scones - See page 15.
- Shortcake - See page 113.

SAUSAGE PINWHEELS

❖ Ingredients:

- COLD Biscuit Dough - See page 9
- Sausage - 1 lb
- Cheddar Cheese - 1 cup
- Flour - 1 tbl

❖ Tools:

- Skillet
- Spatula
- Rolling Pin
- Large Bowl
- Cookie Sheet
- Parchment Paper (or not)
- Plastic Wrap
- Sharp Knife

❖ Directions:

- Break up and fry sausage in skillet. After cooked through, allow to cool slightly, pour off excess grease and put sausage onto paper towels. Pat dry with paper towels and allow to cool thoroughly.
- Mix cooled sausage with shredded cheddar cheese and 1 tbl flour and mix well. Set aside.
- Turn the cold biscuit dough out onto a dry, clean and floured surface and roll out to a large rectangle approximately 1/4-1/2" thick.
- Sprinkle the sausage mixture over the biscuit dough leaving 1" around the edge.
- Starting with the long side, roll it up and seal the edge. Roll into plastic wrap and seal tightly.
- Place in the freezer for at least 30 minutes.
- When ready to prepare, heat oven to 375 degrees and cover the cookie sheet with parchment paper.
- Unwrap the sausage roll from the plastic wrap and cut 1-1 1/2" slices with a sharp, wet knife.
- Place on the cookie sheet about 1" apart and bake until the desired color is achieved (15-20 minutes).

Note: Do not put in an oven that has not been fully preheated. Those crunchy brown bottoms are a favorite for very few. Also, make a big batch and freeze the ones you do not need, saving them for another day.

SAUSAGE BALLS

Sausage Balls were at every party that I attended growing up. We would actually ask people to sign up for dishes in order to ward off having 5 variations of sausage balls at the parties! Again, these can be "enhanced" by adding pepper flakes (although you will not need those if you use hot sausage), chopped jalapeños, etc. Make it yours!

❖ Ingredients:

- Dry Biscuit Dough Mix - 2 c flour, 1 tbl sugar, 4 tsp baking powder, 1 tsp salt and 1 stick (8 tbl) butter "cut in"
- Flour - 1 tbl
- Sausage - 1 lb
- Cheddar Cheese - 1 cup
- Milk - 1/2 cup

❖ Tools:

- Skillet
- Spatula
- Medium Bowl
- Cookie Sheet
- Parchment Paper (or not)

❖ Directions:

- Preheat oven to 375 degrees and cover cookie sheet with parchment paper.
- Break up and fry sausage in skillet. After cooked through, allow to cool slightly, pour off excess grease and put sausage onto paper towels. Pat dry with paper towels and allow to cool thoroughly.
- Mix cooled sausage and shredded cheddar cheese with dry biscuit dough mix.
- Add milk a little at a time and mix with a fork. The mixture will still be a little dry. That's okay.
- Form 1" balls with damp hands and place on the baking sheet with a little space between each ball. Bake for 15-20 minutes or until nice and golden brown.

BLUEBERRY SCONES

Grandad (there is only one of him so no surname is needed to identify who I am talking about) LOVED blueberries. Anytime I was lucky enough to have him to breakfast, I tried to make sure to have at least one item with blueberries. Lord, I miss that man. He was a great hulk of a man that would melt you with his hugs and terrify you witless when you misbehaved. He is the man that my husband modeled himself after and I am so grateful for that every day. So Grandad, this one is for you.

❖ Ingredients:

- All Purpose Flour - 2 cups Sifted + a lil extra
- Sugar - 2 tbl
- Salt - 1 tsp
- Baking Powder - 4 tsp
- Butter - 1 and 1/2 sticks COLD (12 tbl)
- Milk - 3/4 cup
- Vanilla Extract - 1/2 tsp
- Egg - 1 lightly beaten
- Blueberries - 1 pint clean and dry
- Lemon Zest (optional)

❖ Tools:

- Pastry Cutter (or 2 butter knives)
- Measuring Cup and Measuring Spoons
- Mixing Spatula
- Whisk
- Large Bowl
- Cookie Sheet
- Parchment Paper (or not)

❖ Directions:

- Preheat oven to 400 degrees and cover cookie sheet with parchment paper.
- Mix the dry ingredients together. Cut your COLD butter into pats and then add to the dry mix. Using your pastry cutter (or two knives), cut the butter into the dry mix until you have a fine crumble.
- Add blueberries to taste (and optional lemon zest if desired) - be sure not to get too aggressive with the blueberries as their water content can affect the outcome.
- Combine your wet ingredients in a separate small bowl and blend thoroughly before adding slowly and gently to your dry mix. Blend this all together until just blended.
- Throw a little flour out on your counter top (clean please) and dump your mixture out onto the flour. The mixture is going to be sticky so sprinkle a little extra on top to help you manage the dough and, being super gentle, fold, knead, fold, knead and press out to the desired thickness with your fingers.
- Now, you can cut these little buggers out with a knife in a traditional triangle shape or you can use your biscuit cutter or ... just about anything else. Be creative. Make it special.
- Place the cut scones on the parchment covered baking sheet, sprinkle with a little sugar and place in the oven for 10-20 minutes based on the size and thickness. Keep an eye on them for doneness.

Serving Suggestions: Serve plain or with a simple icing made with Confectioner Sugar, Vanilla Flavoring, softened Butter and a dash of Milk (or for a little zing substitute fresh lemon juice for the milk).

SPICED PUMPKIN SCONES

For my friend, Patty. She loves these things and looks everywhere for them starting with the beginning of Fall. Being a good friend (I DO try), I make these for her on occasion. You will LOVE them!

❖ Glaze Ingredients:

- Powdered Sugar - 1 c
- Pumpkin Purée - 1 tbl
- Salt - 1/2 tsp
- Cinnamon - 1/4 tsp
- Ginger - 1/8 tsp
- Cloves - 1/8 tsp
- Nutmeg - 1/8 tsp
- Half and Half - 1 1/2 tbl

❖ Tools:

- Pastry Cutter (or 2 butter knives)
- Measuring Cup and Measuring Spoons
- Mixing Spatula
- Whisk
- Large Bowl
- Cookie Sheet
- Parchment Paper (or not)

❖ Scone Ingredients:

- All Purpose Flour - 2 cups sifted + a lil extra
- Brown Sugar - 1/3 c
- Salt - 1/2 tsp
- Baking Powder - 1 tsp
- Baking Soda - 1/2 tsp
- Cinnamon - 1 tsp
- Ginger - 3/4 tsp
- Cloves - 3/4 tsp
- Nutmeg - 1/2 tsp
- Butter - 1 stick COLD (8 tbl)
- Half and Half - 3 tbl
- Vanilla Extract - 2 tsp
- Egg - 1 lightly beaten
- Molasses - 1 tbl
- Pumpkin Purée - 1/2 c

❖ Directions:

- Heat oven to 400 degrees.
- Line a baking sheet with Parchment Paper.
- Blend the dry ingredients together.
- Cut the COLD butter into the dry mix.
- Mix the wet ingredients together.
- Blend the wet ingredients into the dry.
- Move dough to a clean and floured surface and gently knead 4-5 times until it is smooth.
- Pat the dough into a rectangle about 1/2" thick and cut into squares and then into triangles.
- Bake for 10 - 15 minutes and then cool before glazing.
- Blend all the glaze ingredients together (add more powdered sugar if too thin).
- Using a spoon, drizzle the glaze over the cooled scones.

SCRAMBLED EGGS

Okay. SCRAMBLED EGGS. You would think this would be pretty self explanatory right? Apparently not, since so many really make a mess of scrambled eggs. In fairness, some like their eggs dry, wet, slightly scrambled or (like me) thoroughly blended until you have a beautiful, golden, smooth substance. I am not sure ANYBODY likes brown, crunchy scrambled eggs! The directions below will result in golden, fluffy scrambled eggs. Hope that is your jam!

❖ Ingredients:

- Eggs - 6 at room temperature
- Salt - to taste
- Pepper - to taste
- Butter - 1 tbl
- Olive Oil - 1 tbl

❖ Tools:

- Non-Stick Skillet
- Spatula
- Bowl
- Whisk (or a fork)

❖ Directions:

- Break eggs into a bowl.
- Add desired salt and pepper (go easy ... you can always add more later to taste) and whisk gently until smooth.
- Heat butter and olive oil over medium low heat in skillet.
- Add eggs to the skillet and stir gently with spatula until cooked to the desired doneness. Enjoy!!

Hint: The olive oil when combined with the butter helps the eggs to get fluffy.

OMELETS

OMELETS. I have to admit that this dish drives me crazy because I cannot make an omelet without making a huge mess. However, I occasionally make one because my hubby really likes them and I like him being happy. So, here we go. I clearly do not have the one handed omelet flipping technique perfected so I will share what I do and ask for forgiveness from the "profs".

❖ Ingredients:

- Eggs - 6 at room temperature
- Salt - to taste
- Pepper - to taste
- Butter - 1 tbl
- Olive Oil - 1 tbl
- Chopped Herbs (if desired)

❖ Tools:

- Medium Non-Stick Skillet
- Spatulas (Mixing and Turning)
- Bowl
- Whisk (or a fork)

❖ Directions:

- Break eggs into a bowl.
- Add desired salt and pepper (go easy ... you can always add more later to taste) and any herbs you might want to add and whisk gently until smooth.
- Heat butter and olive oil over medium low heat in skillet.
- Add mixed eggs to the skillet and let them cook without disturbing them until the edges begin to cook and thicken.
- Using your mixing spatula, lift the edges and tilt the pan to allow runny eggs to run underneath.
- When there are almost no runny eggs on top, use your turning spatula to flip the whole thing and be prepared to be splattered!
- Add your favorite ingredients, fold over, plate and enjoy!

EGGS OVER

Not a fan of scrambled eggs? Don't like 'em because you were tortured as a child by variations that were meant to imitate a Bible parable? Mom's attempt to feed the masses with "2 eggs" (my Mom will argue that it is possible if the two eggs come from a goose). Not my fave either but I gotcha covered. Directions can be found on this and the next page for sunny side up and BROTHER RICK'S "OVER" EGGS.

❖ Ingredients:

- Eggs - at room temperature
- Salt - to taste
- Pepper - to taste
- Butter - 1 tbl

❖ Tools:

- Medium Non-Stick Skillet
- Spatula

❖ Directions:

- Crack eggs separately into a bowl (always a bowl first). Trust me on this. You DO NOT want to crack a rotten egg directly into a hot skillet. No rotten eggs? Okay, you are good to go.
- Heat butter over medium low heat in skillet.
- Slide each egg separately into the skillet and keep separated.
- Cook until the whites are the desired doneness and then gently flip and cook until you are too hungry to wait any longer. Slide to your plate and Enjoy!!

SUNNY-SIDE UP EGGS

For those of you who really enjoy looking that yolk right in the eye, sunny-side up eggs. You would think that this would be the easiest preparation, but it can be challenging to cook the whites without over cooking the yolks. My advice here would be to really keep an eye on it.

❖ Ingredients:

- Eggs - at room temperature
- Salt - to taste
- Pepper - to taste
- Butter - 1 tbl

❖ Tools:

- Medium Non-Stick Skillet with a Glass Lid*
- Spatula

❖ Directions:

- Crack eggs separately into a bowl (always a bowl first). Trust me on this. You DO NOT want to crack a rotten egg directly into a hot skillet. No rotten eggs? Okay, you are good to go.
- Heat butter over medium low heat in skillet.
- Slide eggs into the skillet and cover tightly with a glass lid (so you can keep an eye on them) or add enough butter to the skillet to allow you to baste those babies to the desired doneness.
- Cook until the whites are the desired doneness. Slide to your plate and enjoy!!

* You can also add several more tablespoons of butter to the skillet and use the hot melted butter to baste the top of the egg.

EGG IN A HOLE

EGG IN A HOLE. This is exactly what you think it is. Normally, you will find it as an egg cooked in the hole of a slice of bread. However, MY hunny bunny has made improvement suggestions for this (his favorite breakfast dish) that have made it much more fun. While the recipe below is the traditional variety, you can substitute pancakes, bagel slices, french toast, and even a Beyond Meat burger (no kidding) for the bread slices.

❖ Ingredients:

- Eggs - at room temperature
- Bread Slices (or a substitute) - 6
- Salt - to taste
- Pepper - to taste
- Butter - 1-2 tbl

❖ Tools:

- Medium Non-Stick Skillet
- Spatula
- Biscuit Cutter (Small)

❖ Directions:

- Heat butter in skillet over medium-low heat.
- While skillet is heating, use your biscuit cutter to cut holes in the center of your bread slices.
- Working in batches, add bread slices to the heated skillet, break eggs into the center and cook until golden brown on both sides and desired egg "doneness". Serve immediately.

BREAKFAST SAUSAGE CASSEROLE

❖ Ingredients:

- Butter (of course)
- Bread - 1/2 loaf
- Pork Sausage - 1 lb (I like it SPICY)
- Sharp Cheddar - 12 oz
- Half and Half - 1 c
- Milk - 1 c
- Dry Mustard - 1 tsp
- Salt - 1 tsp
- Pepper - dash
- Eggs - 7 at room temperature

❖ Tools:

- 9x13 Baking Dish
- Medium Bowl
- Skillet
- Spatula
- Whisk
- Measuring Cups
- Measuring Spoons
- Aluminum Foil
- Paper Towels

❖ Directions:

- Butter 9x13 baking dish
- Tear the bread into 1-2" pieces
- Break up and brown sausage in a skillet over medium heat until fully cooked.
- Remove the sausage from the skillet and blot with paper towels to remove excess grease.
- In a medium bowl, blend together the eggs, half and half, milk, dry mustard, salt and pepper.
- To compose, put bread in the bottom of the buttered baking dish. Cover this with the cooked sausage. Next, sprinkle liberally with the cheese and pour the egg mixture over the whole shebang.
- Cover with aluminum foil and refrigerate overnight (or NOT ... I couldn't wait that long).
- Bake covered at 350 degrees for 50 minutes.
- Remove aluminum foil and bake another 15 minutes. If you like the top crunchy (my man DOES), hit that thing with the broiler for a few minutes.

Enjoy!

BREAKFAST SKILLET

Want something pretty simple to cook and don't mind some knife work? Try this one dish breakfast skillet!

❖ Ingredients:

- Onion - 1/2 Medium
- Bell Pepper - 1 Medium
- Jalapeño - 1 Medium
- Bacon - 4 Slices
- Potato - 1 Medium
- Baby Spinach - 1 Container
- Eggs - 6 at Room Temperature
- Cheddar Cheese - 1 Cup Shredded
- Olive Oil - 1 tbl
- Salt - to taste
- Pepper - to taste

❖ Tools:

- Cutting Board
- Sharp Knife
- Medium Non-Stick Oven Safe Skillet
- Oven Mitts (or a towel or your husband)
- Medium Mixing Bowl

❖ Directions:

- Prep the vegetables. Medium dice the onion and bell pepper. Seed and de-vein the jalapeño and dice. Peel and dice the potato. Make sure the spinach is clean and dry.
- Cut the bacon into 1/2" strips.
- Heat olive oil over medium to medium low heat until hot but not smoking. Add potato, onion, bacon and jalapeño to the skillet. Salt and pepper to taste and cook until potato begins to soften and the bacon is crispy.
- Add spinach and allow to wilt slightly before stirring. Continue to stir and cook until spinach is wilted and incorporated well.
- Crack eggs into a bowl (we are always checking these out). If "all good," create a little well in the center of your skillet and gently slide the eggs into the skillet wells and over the vegetables. Allow to cook without stirring until the eggs begin to set.
- Sprinkle cheddar cheese over top liberally. Place in the oven under the broiler until bubbly. Remove and allow to sit for a couple of minutes before serving.

Serving Suggestion: Serve with salsa and sour cream.

FRITTATA

❖ Ingredients:

- Shallot - 1 Small
- Bell Pepper - 1 Small
- Asparagus - 1/2 Small Bunch
- Eggs - 6
- Heavy Cream - 1/2 Cup
- Fresh Thyme - 1 tbl Chopped
- Parmesan Cheese - 3/4 Cup Shredded
- Butter - 1 tbl
- Olive Oil - 1 tbl
- Salt - to taste
- Pepper - to taste

❖ Tools:

- Cutting Board
- Sharp Knife
- Medium Non-Stick Oven Safe Skillet
- Oven Mitts (or a towel or your husband)
- Medium Mixing Bowl
- Egg Whip (or a fork)

❖ Directions:

- Prep the vegetables. Peel and dice the shallot. De-vein, seed and small dice the bell pepper. Clean and dry the asparagus then trim 1" off the bottom and cut into 1" pieces.
- Heat olive oil and butter over medium to medium low heat until hot but not smoking.
- Add diced/cut vegetables to the skillet. Salt and pepper to taste and cook until vegetables begin to soften.
- While the vegetables are cooking, crack eggs into a bowl, add heavy cream, chopped Thyme, salt and pepper and blend with an egg whip until blended thoroughly.
- Pour the egg mixture evenly over the vegetables in the skillet and allow to cook without stirring until the edges set.
- Sprinkle Parmesan cheese over top liberally and place in the oven under the broiler until bubbly.
- Remove and allow to sit for a couple of minutes before serving.

Serving Suggestion: Serve with side salad and biscuits.

SPANISH EGGS IN A BASKET

My husband and I have noticed as we get older that we crave things with a little more flavor. Maybe our taste buds are dying a slow death like our old bodies. This has pushed us toward things with much more spice. The following recipe is a spin on Huevos Rancheros. There are a lot of variations that you can try and I will do my best to outline what a few of these options might be. Again, be creative and modify to suit your personal tastes.

❖ Ingredients:

- Shallot - 1 Small
- Black Beans - 1 Can Drained and Rinsed
- Fire Roasted Tomato - 1 Can
- Taco Sauce - 1 Small Jar
- Cumin - 2 tsp
- Garlic - 1 Clove
- Garlic Salt - 1/2 tsp
- Fresh Thyme - 1 tbl Chopped
- Cheddar Cheese - 1 Cup Shredded
- Eggs - 4
- 6" Corn Tortillas - 4
- Instant Rice - 1 Cup
- Avocado - 2 Ripe
- Cilantro - 1/4 Cup Chopped
- Water - 3/4 Cup
- Olive Oil - 1 tbl
- Salt - to taste
- Pepper - to taste

❖ Tools:

- Cutting Board
- Sharp Knife
- Medium Skillet
- Oven Mitts (or a towel or your husband)
- Small Mixing Bowl
- Oven Safe Ramekins - 4

❖ Directions:

- Preheat the oven to 375 degrees.
- Mix the fire roasted tomatoes and 1/2 c of the taco sauce in a bowl and set aside.
- Spray the ramekins with cooking spray.
- Wrap the corn tortillas in plastic wrap and heat in the microwave for 20-30 seconds.
- Brush each side of the corn tortillas with a little olive oil and carefully lay inside the ramekins. Set aside. (Continued on next page)

❖ Directions: (Continued)

- Prepare the rice according to the box instructions. When cooked, add 1/2 c of the tomato mixture, blend and cover.
- Peel and dice the shallot and chop the Thyme.
- Heat olive oil over medium to medium low heat until hot but not smoking.
- Add diced shallot to skillet and cook until slightly brown.
- Add diced garlic and cumin to skillet and sauté for 20-30 seconds.
- Add garlic salt, black beans and 3/4 c water to the skillet and, using a potato ricer, mash and stir until it thickens.
- Put a layer of the tomato rice onto the tortilla, add a layer of black bean mash, create a hole in the middle with the back of a spoon and drop in an egg.
- Spoon the remaining tomato mixture over the top, sprinkle with cheese and bake for 15 minutes. Broil for an additional 2-3 minutes and serve with sliced or mashed avocado and chopped cilantro.

PANCAKES

C'mon, y'all. Give up the pre-made mix and give this a try. I promise you will love 'em!

❖ Ingredients:

- Flour - 1 c
- Sugar - 1 tbl
- Baking Powder - 3 tsp
- Salt - 1/2 tsp
- 1 Egg - Slightly Beaten
- Melted Butter - 2 tbl + Extra for Cooking
- Milk - 3/4 - 1 c

❖ Tools:

- Medium Skillet or Griddle
- Mixing Bowl
- Measuring Cups and Spoons
- Whisk
- Turning and Mixing Spatulas

❖ Directions:

- Mix dry ingredients.
- Add wet ingredients (make sure melted butter has cooled) adding enough milk to reach desired consistency (more milk creates thinner pancakes).
- Heat skillet/griddle to medium low, melting 1-2 tbl butter.
- Using a 1/4 c measuring cup, scoop up batter and pour onto skillet/griddle. Turn when bubbles begin to appear and pop and the edges begin to dry. Cook until edges are dry and/or crispy.
- Serve with butter, syrup, jelly, etc.

For Bacon Pancakes: Cook up a whole mess of bacon nice and crispy and then put back in the skillet and pour pancake batter over the strips and cook as usual. Or, fry up some nice sausage links and rolls those little babies up in your pancakes. Oh, so yummy!

LEIPER'S FORK
DISTILLERY

FRENCH TOAST

This is a recipe that you can really play with. You can use different types of bread (plain white or wheat bread, ciabatta, french, etc) and add spices to elevate it. This recipe is your basic recipe but I encourage you to experiment with adding cinnamon or other spices and varying the bread types.

❖ Ingredients:

- 6 Eggs
- 3/4 c Milk
- Ciabatta Bread (6 Thick Slices)
- Butter - 4 tbl
- Sugar - 1 tbl
- Salt - 1/4 tsp
- Flour - 1/4 c
- Vanilla Extract - 1/2 tsp

❖ Tools:

- Medium Skillet
- Mixing Bowl
- Whisk
- Large Shallow Dish
- Turning Spatula

❖ Directions:

- Mix dry ingredients.
- Whisk together the eggs, milk and vanilla extract. Blend in the dry ingredients.
- Lay bread slices in a single layer in a shallow dish and pour egg blend over making sure that all bread surfaces are covered.
- Cover with plastic wrap and refrigerate until liquid is completely absorbed (I sometimes leave them overnight).
- Heat butter in skillet over medium-low heat. Add soaked bread slices to hot skillet and cook until golden brown on both sides (5-8 min on each side) working in batches as needed.

Serving Suggestions: Sprinkle with cinnamon sugar or powdered sugar or serve with syrup.

WAFFLES

You can do this! Skip the mix and make 'em from scratch! You in?

❖ Ingredients:

- Flour - 2 c
- Sugar - 1 tbl
- Baking Powder - 4 tsp
- Salt - 1/2 tsp
- 2 Eggs - Slightly Beaten
- Melted Butter - 1/2 c
- Milk - 1 3/4 c

❖ Tools:

- Waffle Iron (non-stick!)
- Mixing Bowl
- Measuring Cups and Spoons
- Whisk
- Mixing Spatulas

❖ Directions:

- Mix dry ingredients.
- Add wet ingredients (make sure melted butter has cooled) and mix well.
- Heat waffle iron (if not using a waffle iron with a non-stick surface, use cooking spray on cooking surfaces).
- Using a measuring cup, scoop up batter (1/2 to 2/3 c) and pour onto center of hot waffle iron. Cook until indicated or until steaming stops.
- Serve with butter, syrup, jelly, etc.

NO SYRUP? TRY JAM!

Alrighty then. Time for a childhood story. When Mom would make pancakes, we would buzz the kitchen like dive bombing Seagulls attempting to lift a fresh pancake from the pile. It was an exercise in frustration since my Mom (like most all moms) has eyes in the back of her head and would scoot the plate out of reach just as you thought you had one. By the time those pancakes finally hit the table we were a fair way to starving. Imagine waiting patiently just to be told as your mouth is watering that “oh yeah, there is no syrup.” WAIT!!! Please tell me it ain’t so! “No syrup?” I complain. “No syrup. Eat ’em with jelly and be happy!” accompanied by a pop on the back of my head. Sometimes, choices are just that easy.

The lesson here is not to be constrained by what is “normally” done. Be creative! Try blackberry jam on those pancakes (or waffles). You will be glad you did.

CHEESY GRITS CASSEROLE

Grits are actually simple. If you just want to make plain grits, you can do that easily by just using the instructions on the container. The great thing about grits is that they are so versatile. For a breakfast dish, make plain grits and add either butter and sugar or salt and pepper and just eat them with toast. For a dinner dish, like Shrimp and Grits, you can make them savory with the addition of spices and/or cheese. MY FAVORITE, a cheesy grit casserole, can be used as a side dish with almost anything.

❖ Ingredients:

- White Hominy Grits - 1 c (dry)
- Milk - 2 c
- Water - 2 c
- Salt - 1 tsp
- Pepper - 1/4 tsp
- Paprika - 1/4 tsp
- 2 Eggs - Slightly Beaten
- Shredded Sharp Cheddar Cheese - 1 1/2 c
- Butter - 2 tbl

❖ Tools:

- Loaf Pan (or 1 1/2 quart casserole dish)
- Medium Saucepan
- Measuring Cups and Measuring Spoons
- Whisk
- Mixing Spatulas

❖ Directions:

- Heat oven to 350 degrees.
- Butter bottom and sides of Loaf Pan.
- Heat to boiling milk, water, salt and pepper in saucepan. Gradually add grits stirring constantly and reduce heat to simmer. Keep stirring until the grits start to thicken. When they have thickened, add the cheese and blend thoroughly.
- Beat the eggs in the now empty 2 c measuring cup. Add 1 cup of the hot mixture to your eggs in the measuring cup and mix thoroughly. Return the contents of the measuring cup to the saucepan and blend in with the remaining cheesy grits.
- Pour the whole thing into your loaf pan, sprinkle with paprika, dot with butter, and bake until it sets (35-50 minutes - depends on your baking dish). Let stand for 15 minutes after removing from oven.

BREAKFAST POTATOES

HASHBROWN POTATOES

❖ Ingredients:

- Potato - 3 Medium
- Canola Oil - 4 tbl
- Salt and Pepper - To Taste

❖ Tools:

- Medium Skillet (I prefer my cast iron)
- Metal Turning Spatula
- Grater Box

❖ Directions:

- Peel and shred potatoes (with large side of grater box).
- Place shredded potato in a colander and run cold water over the potato until it runs clear. Place on paper towels and dry as thoroughly as possible.
- Heat oil in skillet over medium heat until hot but not smoking.
- Add potatoes in a single layer and sprinkle with salt and pepper. Allow to cook untouched for 3-5 minutes (until the bottom starts to become crunchy). Using a turning spatula, cut the potato into quarters in the skillet and flip the quarters. Continue to cook untouched until flipped side is crunchy. Remove to a paper towel, pat to remove excess oil and serve immediately.

BREAKFAST POTATOES / HOME FRIES

❖ Ingredients:

- Potato - 3 Medium
- Canola Oil - 4 tbl
- Salt and Pepper - To Taste
- Onion - 1 Sliced (optional)

❖ Tools:

- Medium Skillet (I prefer my cast iron)
- Metal Turning Spatula

❖ Directions:

- Clean potatoes and pierce with a fork. Place in a microwave and cook for 2 minutes per potato (for 3 potatoes cook 6 minutes).
- Allow to cool for 10 minutes. Remove peel and either large dice or slice, whatever your preference.
- Heat oil in skillet over medium heat until hot but not smoking.
- Add potatoes in a single layer (add optional onion) and sprinkle with salt and pepper. Cover and allow to cook untouched for 5 minutes (until the bottom starts to become crunchy). Flip, cover and allow to cook for an additional 5 minutes. Flip and cook uncovered until you reach your desired level of doneness and crunchiness. Remove to a paper towel, pat to remove excess oil and serve immediately.

COUNTRY HAM AND RED EYE GRAVY

Oh my GOODNESS. I cannot tell you how many people I meet who have never had Red Eye Gravy. I can report that not a single person I have ever prepared this for has not liked it. It is unusual for sure, but it is absolutely DELICIOUS when served over biscuits or a grits-based dish that I will share below as a serving suggestion.

❖ Ingredients:

- Bone In Sliced Country Ham
- Cold Regular Brewed Coffee - 1/2 c (I like to use day old coffee)
- Water - 1/2 c
- Butter - 1 tbl
- Beef Bouillon - 1 tbl

❖ Tools:

- Large Skillet (I prefer my cast iron)
- Wooden Spoon
- Sharp Knife or Kitchen Scissors

❖ Directions:

- Cut the fat edges of your country ham with a knife or kitchen scissors at about 2" intervals. This prevents the country ham from curling up when cooking.
- Place a couple pieces of the country ham in your skillet and turn your stove on to medium (medium-low works best for me if I am on a gas range). Allow the country ham to cook until it begins to caramelize before turning. Your ham is already "cooked" so we are just trying to add a little crunch and warmth to each side.
- Working in batches, finish cooking all of your country ham, removing it to a plate when done.
- Now, for the gravy. Add the coffee and water to the now empty skillet and using a wooden spoon work the bottom of that pan until all the little country ham pieces that stuck to the skillet are loosened. Add the butter and bouillon and stir to dissolve. Taste, modify, taste, modify. Serve!

Serving Suggestions: 1) Over biscuits with some eggs and country ham for sides. 2) Build this: A layer of Grits (cheesy or plain) covered with a large piece of country ham, 2 sunny side up eggs and topped with Red Eye Gravy. Yum!

THE HAM...

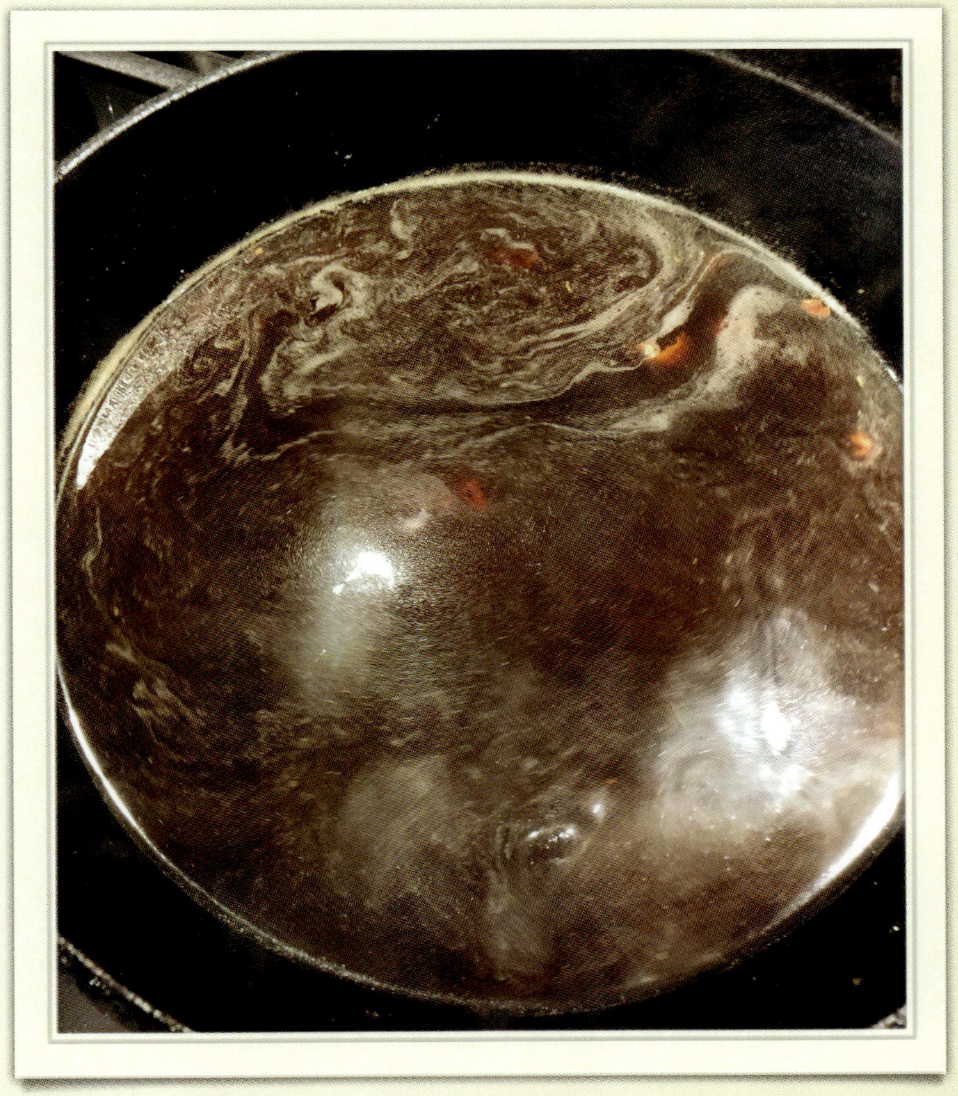

...AND THE GRAVY!

MILK GRAVY

We can put gravy on almost anything and make a meal out of it: Biscuits and Gravy, Toast and Gravy, Mashed Potato and Gravy (this is MY favorite). We make it from the fat left in a skillet after cooking meat. I know. This sounds disgusting but, trust me, this is delicious. The most commonly made gravies are made from the drippings remaining after cooking Bacon, Sausage, Fried Chicken or Fried Pork Chops. The instructions are the same. It is just the "fat" source that changes the flavor. To make gravy successfully, you are going to have to commit to a little experimentation. The most difficult part is judging how much flour you are going to use and this is based on how much "fat" you have in the pan.

❖ Ingredients:

- The fat remaining in the skillet after the preparation of Bacon, Sausage or Chicken/ Pork Chops
- Flour (approx 1/3-1/2 c), Milk, Salt & Pepper

❖ Tools:

- Medium Skillet (I prefer my cast iron)
- Large Fork
- Measuring Cup

❖ Directions:

- Before you begin, know this: You are going to want to make your gravy as soon as (or very shortly after) you remove your meat from the skillet and you are almost always going to use more milk than you think and less flour than you think. I usually mix 1/3-1/2 c flour with salt and pepper to taste and set it aside. I take out the milk carton, remove the top (trust me ... this goes fast and you will need that milk ready to go) and set it aside. Now, heat the "fat" you have in the skillet over medium to medium-low heat until it is hot but not smoking. Slowly, add your flour/salt/pepper mixture a little at a time while stirring constantly with the back, flat side of your fork. Your job here is to make a smooth, thin paste that you continue to stir until it starts to brown (the browning gives it better flavor). When you reach a light brown color, start adding milk while you continue to stir. It will thicken VERY quickly so you might as well keep that milk carton in your hand until this part is done.
- Now, somewhere in here between stirring and managing your milk carton, you need to remove the skillet from the heat. The gravy will continue to thicken. Just keep adding milk and stirring until you reach YOUR desired thickness. Now ... taste, modify, taste, modify. Serve!

Note: Earlier, I told you that you would want to keep your left over bacon fat (when you are not making gravy or you just have more fat left than you need). The following is one of the reasons WHY we keep a supply tightly sealed in our fridge. There are going to be days when you will want a little bacon gravy but you will not want bacon. Voilà! Dig right into the middle of that bacon fat from the fridge, digging out a nice large spoonful making sure to go through all the layers so you gather the "flavor layers" and plop that in your skillet. Heat that up and you are ready to go!

Mains

FRIED CHICKEN

This recipe is specific to chicken, but I also use it to make fried pork chops, minute steaks, etc. When you are done you ABSOLUTELY MUST use the skillet remainders to make the white chicken gravy for the mashed potatoes that I KNOW you are serving with that yummy chicken.

❖ Ingredients:

- Chicken (I like bone in Breasts)
- Flour - 1 1/2 c
- Salt - 1 tsp
- Pepper - 1/2 tsp
- Paprika - 1/2 tsp
- Eggs - 2 lightly beaten
- Milk - 1/4 c
- Canola Oil - 1/2 - 1 c

❖ Tools:

- Medium Skillet with Lid (I prefer my cast iron)
- Tongs
- Wide Shallow Mixing Bowl
- Shallow Plate with a Lip
- Measuring Cup and Spoons

❖ Directions:

- Mix dry ingredients and put on plate.
- Mix eggs and milk in the mixing bowl (this is your egg wash) and set it alongside your flour plate.
- Rinse off your chicken and pat dry with a kitchen towel or paper towels.
- Add enough canola oil to your skillet to give you approximately 1/2" and heat the oil over medium heat until hot but not smoking.
- While the oil is heating, dip your chicken in the egg wash, coat in flour, dip in egg wash, coat in flour again and place in hot skillet (CAREFULLY!).
- Cook until light brown on both sides (about 8-10 minutes) then cover tightly and simmer on low until the thickest pieces are cooked through (maybe another 20-30 minutes).
- Remove cover and cook for another 5-10 minutes turning occasionally to allow the chicken to crisp up. Remove to a paper towel covered plate.

Note: Add/change oil as needed if you are cooking in batches.

CHICKEN POT PIE

I LOVE this dish and so does my sweet pea. It may seem pretty daunting but is actually not a difficult dish to prepare AND you have the option using pre-cooked pulled chicken from your local grocer and topping it with "whop" biscuits instead of a pie crust if you are short on time. You can also play with your veggie additions. My husband HATES peas so this version is "pealess" just for him.

❖ Ingredients:

- Chicken - 2 large skinless/boneless
- Chicken Broth - 4 c
  (I LOVE Bone Broth)
- Chicken Bouillon - 1 tbl + more to taste
- Butter - 12 tbl
- Flour - 3/4 c
- Heavy Cream - 1/4 c
- Onion - 1 large
- Carrots - 2 medium
- Celery - 2 medium stalks
- Potato - 1 medium
- Fresh Parsley - 1/4 c (optional)
- Pie Crust (see page 96)

❖ Tools:

- 2 Medium Sauce Pans
- Deep Dish Pie Plate
- Cookie Sheet
- Cutting Board
- Sharp Knife
- Whisk
- Measuring Cups and Spoons

❖ Directions:

- Preheat oven to 375 degrees. Prepare and refrigerate your pie crust.
- Small dice Onion, Potato, Carrot and Celery.
- Place raw chicken in a medium pan and cover with water. Boil till done through (approximately 10-15 minutes). You should check doneness by cutting through the thickest part of the largest piece. When done, remove to a plate to cool and discard water. (DO NOT over cook your chicken. It will be tough.) When cool, either shred or cut to small bite size pieces.
- In the same pan, warm your chicken broth and add the bouillon heating until it is dissolved. Remove from heat to cool. Break out that tasting spoon! If the flavor is not to your liking, add more broth or bouillon.
- Next, in a separate pan, melt your butter over medium low heat. Add your onion and cook 8-10 minutes until onion begins to soften and becomes translucent. Slowly add your flour and stir constantly for 1-2 minutes until the mixture is smooth. Now, slowly add your chicken broth stirring with a whisk until all of the broth is incorporated. Continue to cook until the mixture begins to thicken. Add your chicken, carrots, celery, potato and parsley and stir until all is coated. Break out that tasting spoon again and add salt/pepper to taste. I have found that dishes with potatoes sometimes require a little extra salt but this is YOUR CALL. Cover and remove from the heat.
- Roll out your pie crust to 3" beyond the diameter of the pie plate (I usually just sit my pie plate upside down on the rolled out dough to judge) and cut away the excess. Fill your pie plate with your Pot Pie filling and top with the pie crust being sure to seal the edges to the pie plate. Cut 3 small holes in the top of the crust, sprinkle the top with pepper and sea salt (I love finishing salt), put the whole thing on a cookie sheet and bake for 50 minutes to 1 hour (until the crust is a golden brown).

Note: You WILL have bubble over with this so do not forget your cookie sheet!

CHICKEN N DUMPLINGS

This dish was a mainstay of my childhood. It requires time if you want to boil your own chicken to make your own broth, but it can be made fairly quickly with some store bought ingredients. You can choose YOUR way with two prep options below.

❖ Broth Ingredients:

Grandma Gayle's Way

- Broiler/Fryer Chicken - 3 - 3 1/2 lb
- Water - 4 c
- Salt - 1 1/2 tsp
- Pepper - 1/2 tsp
- Onion - 1 small
- Carrots - 1 medium
- Celery - 1 medium stalks
- Fresh Parsley - 1/4 c (optional)

"Speed It Up" Way

- Chicken Bone Broth - 4 c
- Chicken Bouillon - 2 tbl
  (I like "Better Than Bouillon")
- 1 Store Bought Roasted Chicken

❖ Broth Directions:

Grandma Gayle's Way

- Remove anything packed inside chicken and discard (or boil separately for later use).
- Place chicken in dutch oven, add onion, carrot, celery, salt, pepper, parsley and water.
- Heat until boiling, skim off foam, reduce heat to simmer, cover and cook for about 45 minutes (or until legs just about fall off).
- Remove from heat and allow to cool until just warm.
- Remove chicken to a plate and strain broth to remove vegetables.
- Return broth to pan and heat on low while preparing dumplings.

"Speed It Up" Way

- Heat Bone Broth to boiling.
- Dissolve Bouillon in broth.

❖ Dumpling Ingredients:

- Shortening - 3 tbl (I like Crisco)
- Flour - 1 1/2 c
- Baking Powder - 2 tsp
- Salt - 3/4 tsp
- Milk - 3/4 c

❖ Dumpling Directions:

- Mix dry ingredients in a medium bowl.
- Cut shortening into the dry mix until it is fine.
- Add milk and blend.

❖ Dish Composition:

- Remove bones from cooked chicken and discard. Pull the chicken into bite sized pieces.
- Add chicken pieces to boiling broth.
- Drop large tablespoons of dumpling dough into broth.
- Cook uncovered for 5 minutes, reduce heat, cover and simmer an additional 8 minutes.

ROASTED CHICKEN

Now, you can certainly buy a roasted chicken at the grocery these days BUT if you want to "quality control" then you need to know how to roast your own chicken. Back in the day, mom would catch them, wring their necks, pluck and clean them. This is WAY too much for me and there are STORIES about that but I need more therapy before we get into those! This recipe assumes you are using a store bought, raw (and thawed) roasting chicken (and yes, there is a difference).

Uses: Chicken Salad, Chicken Soup, Sandwiches, Dressing, etc.

❖ Ingredients:

- Roasting Chicken - 3 - 3 1/2 lb
- Butter - 4 tbl
- Salt - 1 1/2 tsp
- Pepper - 1/2 tsp

❖ Tools:

- Roasting Pan

❖ Directions:

- Preheat oven to 375 degrees.
- Remove anything stuffed inside the bird's cavity and discard (or save for a gravy prep).
- Rinse the bird with cold water and pat dry.
- Place the chicken breast side up on a roasting rack.
- Brush with melted butter and sprinkle with salt and pepper.
- Bake for 2-2 1/4 hours or until you can easily pull off a leg.
- Remove to a plate and allow to fully cool.

ROASTED CHICKEN N VEG

This dish can be modified to work for the vegetable preferences of almost any family (other than my sister-in-law's as her list of "vegetables" includes Mac and Cheese and Hashbrown Casserole ... did I mention that we are southern and our list of "veggies" can be a little unique?). The versatility works wonderfully for families with gardens as you can change the veg based on what is "in season". With this recipe, I would only work with fresh vegetables. See my favorite version below.

❖ Ingredients:

- Chicken Breasts - 4
- Brussels Sprouts - small pkg
- Turnip - 1 lrg
- Onion - 1 lrg
- Carrot - 1 lrg
- Potato - 1 lrg
- Corn - 1 ear
- Lemon - 1
- Rosemary - 1/2 tsp (fresh if possible)
- Garlic - 2 cloves
- Olive Oil
- Salt and Pepper

❖ Tools:

- Dutch Oven
- Tongs
- Cutting Board
- Peeler
- Sharp Knife
- Large Mixing Bowl

❖ Directions:

- Preheat oven to 425 degrees.
- Rinse chicken and pat dry.
- Clean, peel and chunk dice your turnip, carrot and potato. Clean the Brussels sprouts, remove the outside leaves and halve. Peel, halve and slice the onion. Remove skin from garlic cloves. Shuck, clean and cut your corn cob into quarters. Place all the vegetables in a large mixing bowl, drizzle with olive oil, season with salt, pepper and rosemary and toss to coat.
- Drizzle a little olive oil into the bottom of your dutch oven and add chicken skin side up (ribs down). Drizzle additional olive oil over the chicken and sprinkle with salt, pepper and rosemary.
- Add vegetables to the dutch oven being careful to not completely bury the chicken (the more skin exposed the nicer this will turn out ... hmmm ... yes I am talking about CHICKEN LOL). Place your corn strategically to make sure it is mostly buried. Squeeze the lemon into a cup, remove seeds and pour over the dish.
- Cover with the lid and put in the oven to bake for 35 minutes. Remove lid and allow to bake for an additional 20 to 30 minutes to crisp up the chicken skin and roast the vegetables (you can finish with a short broil if you like).

CHICKEN FRIED STEAK

This is a "nothing to it" dish that we ate a lot in our early years. It is usually served with mashed potatoes, white gravy and another vegetable (or two, depending on how big your man is).

❖ Ingredients:

- Minute (aka Cube) Steaks - 4
- Canola Oil
- Milk - 1/4 c
- Eggs - 2
- Paprika - 1/2 tsp
- Salt - 1 tsp
- Pepper - 1/2 tsp
- Flour - 1 1/2 c

❖ Tools:

- Wide Mixing Bowl
- Shallow Plate with a Lip
- Measuring Cups and Spoons
- Tongs
- Medium to Large Skillet (I like my cast iron for this)

❖ Directions:

- Remove the steaks from the packaging and allow to come to room temperature.
- Mix the dry ingredients together and put them on the plate.
- Lightly whip the eggs and blend in your milk (this is your egg wash) and set this right next to your plate of dry ingredients.
- Add enough canola oil to just coat the bottom of your skillet and heat the skillet over medium-low heat until hot but not smoking.
- While the skillet is heating, coat your steaks in the dry mixture, dip them in the egg wash, coat them again in the dry mixture and then gently place them in your hot skillet.
- Cook until light brown on both sides (about 2 minutes each side).
- Remove to a paper towel covered plate and then serve immediately! This type of steak does not need to "rest"...it needs to be devoured!

Note: Add additional oil as needed if you are cooking in batches.

NOW, use the skillet remainders to make white gravy for the mashed potatoes that I KNOW you are serving with those delicious Chicken Fried Steaks. Also, consider covering that meat with the gravy too.

NANA'S EGG NOODLES

This is my mother-in-law's recipe. My husband LOVES this stuff and asks for it to be made for every holiday meal. I cannot explain why it does not make it on the table more often because it is a simple, filling and delicious one-dish meal. I am boiling the chicken in this recipe but if you are in a time crunch, please feel free to substitute all-white canned chicken!

❖ Ingredients:

- Skinless Chicken Breast - 2 lrg
- Eggs - 2 lrg
- Egg Noodles - 1 lrg Bag
- Cream of Chicken Soup - 2 Cans
- Cream of Mushroom Soup - 1 Can
- Bread Crumbs - 1 c
- Butter - 3 tbl +
- Salt and Pepper - to taste
- Onion - 1/4 c fine diced (optional)

❖ Tools:

- Glass Baking Dish
- 2 Medium Sauce Pans
- Medium Mixing Bowl
- Measuring Cup

❖ Directions:

- Preheat oven to 375 degrees.
- Boil the eggs for 8 minutes. Peel, let cool and slice thinly.
- Add 6 c of water to a sauce pan and boil the chicken until done through (check after 10 minutes by slicing into the chicken center - there should be no pink).
- Let the cooked chicken cool to the touch and then pull or cut it into small pieces (I prefer mine pulled :)).
- Cook the Egg Noodles as directed on the packaging shortening the time by 2 minutes (you do not want soggy noodles and they will be if they are fully cooked when they go in the oven).
- Drain and rinse the Egg Noodles with cool water (to stop the cooking).
- Melt the butter and mix it with the bread crumbs (homemade bread crumbs are delish but store bought will do fine for this simple recipe).
- In your mixing bowl, mix together the noodles, soups, sliced eggs and chicken.
- Transfer the mixture to a buttered baking dish and top with the bread crumb/butter mixture.
- Bake for 20-30 minutes or until the bread crumb topping has browned and the casserole is bubbly.

BAKED FISH

I must confess. I do not normally like, and therefore eat, fish. Long story short, I was force fed fish on a camping trip when I was very young and was so traumatized that just the smell of fish will send me scrambling. However, my husband LOVES fish so I have learned to prepare certain less "fishy" fish. Below is a simple baked fish that he adores (and I manage to like too).

❖ Ingredients:

- Halibut Filets - 4 8oz Filets
- Lemons - 2
- Olive Oil
- Salt and Pepper - to taste

❖ Tools:

- Glass Baking Dish
- Tongs

❖ Directions:

- Preheat oven to 425 degrees.
- Rinse fish and pat dry.
- Drizzle olive oil over both sides of fish and a little in the baking dish. Salt and pepper the fish to taste and place in baking dish flat side (where the skin was) down.
- Squeeze fresh lemon juice over the fish and allow to rest for 15 minutes.
- Bake for 15-20 minutes or until the fish is white and flakes with a fork.

Serving Suggestion: Serve piping hot with sautéed spinach and sliced fresh tomatoes.

Alternate Use: You can also skip the lemon, add ancho chili powder and cumin to your fish seasoning and flake the baked fish to use in fish tacos. Hint: make your own salsa and use corn tortillas that you heat in a skillet or on the grill.

PULLED PORK

❖ Components:

- Corn Cakes (see page 116)
- Vinegar Cole Slaw (see page 87)
- Barbecue/Hot Sauce of Choice
- Pulled Pork (this page)

❖ Pulled Pork Ingredients:

- 3-4 lb Boston Butt Pork Roast (do not remove string)
- Salt & Pepper
- Canola Oil

❖ Tools:

- Dutch Oven

❖ Directions:

- Preheat oven to 325 degrees.
- Liberally coat pork roast with salt and pepper on all sides.
- Heat 2-3 tbl canola oil in the dutch oven on the stove over medium to medium-high heat. Brown the roast on all sides (to seal in those yummy juices).
- Cover and bake for 2 1/2 - 3 hours or until the Pork pulls apart easily with a fork.

❖ Composition:

- Top your corn cake with the pulled pork.
- Add your sauce of choice. Top with slaw and enjoy!

TUNA NOODLE CASSEROLE

❖ Ingredients:

- Tuna – 1 lrg can
- Cream of Mushroom Soup – 1 can
- Cheddar Cheese Soup – 1 can
- Onion – 1 med
- Pimentos – 1 small jar
- Egg Noodles – 8-10 oz bag
- Cheddar Cheese – 8 oz shredded
- Vegetable Oil – 1 tbl
- Milk – 1 c
- Garlic Salt – 1/2 tsp
- Breadcrumbs – 1 1/2 c
- Butter – 4 tbl

❖ Tools:

- Medium Skillet
- Medium Mixing Bowl
- Large Baking Dish
- Medium Saucepan
- Measuring Cups and Spoons

❖ Directions:

- Preheat oven to 350 degrees.
- Drain the tuna.
- Melt the butter. Mix the melted butter with the breadcrumbs and set aside.
- Cook the egg noodles according to the package directions. Do not overcook!
- Drain, rinse with cool water, and set aside.
- Peel and dice onion. Add vegetable oil to skillet and cook diced onion until tender.
- Add the two soups and the pimentos to the skillet with the onions and mix well.
- Let it come to a low boil, then stir in the milk.
- Add the drained tuna and the noodles to the skillet and mix gently. Salt to taste.
- Transfer to a baking dish, sprinkle the bread crumb mixture over the top and bake for 20 minutes. Remove from the oven, sprinkle the cheddar cheese over the top, return to the oven and bake for an additional 15 minutes or until bubbly and the topping crispy.

SALMON CROQUETTES (PATTIES)

I did NOT like fish when I was growing up (yes, there is another traumatic story associated with this particular dislike) but I LOVED these. Just make sure to pick out all the little round bones (unless you happen to like extra crunch in your croquette!

❖ Ingredients:

- Salmon - 2 Cans (remove bones)
- Eggs - 2
- Mayonnaise - 2 tbl
- Worcestershire Sauce - a dash
- Ritz Crackers - 3/4 c crushed
- Bread Crumbs - 1 1/2 c
- Canola Oil

❖ Tools:

- Medium Mixing Bowl
- Mixing and Turning Spatulas
- Measuring Cups and Spoons
- Medium to Large Skillet
  (I like my cast iron for this)

❖ Directions:

- Add salmon to the bowl and flake with a fork. Add lightly beaten egg, mayonnaise and Worcestershire sauce and mix thoroughly.
- Slowly add the crushed Ritz crackers and mix well.
- Form into palm sized patties (unless you have MONSTER hands) and dredge patties in the bread crumbs.
- Add enough canola oil to just coat the bottom of your skillet and heat the skillet over medium low heat until hot but not smoking.
- When the skillet has heated, add the salmon patties and fry until crunchy (2-3 minutes on each side).
- Remove to a paper towel covered plate and then serve immediately!

Serving Suggestion: Serve piping hot with mashed potatoes as a side.

STUFFED BELL PEPPERS

❖ Ingredients:

- Bell Peppers - 6 (Red, Green or Yellow)
- Ground Beef - 1 lb
- Onion - 1/4 c fine diced
- Rice - 1 c cooked
- Salt - 3/4 tsp
- Pepper - 1/2 tsp
- Garlic Salt - 1/4 tsp
- Tomato Sauce - 1 15 oz can
- Mozzarella - 1 c shredded

❖ Tools:

- Medium Skillet
- Large Baking Dish
- Large Pan
- Sharp Knife
- Cutting Board
- Measuring Cups and Spoons

❖ Directions:

- Preheat oven to 350 degrees.
- Cook your rice.
- Wash the peppers. Cut the top off each pepper and remove all seeds and membranes. Cut a thin slice off the bottom (just enough to allow the peppers to sit upright).
- Place the peppers in a large pan and cover with water. Heat to boiling and cook for 3 minutes.
- Remove the peppers from the water and place upright in the baking dish.
- Cook beef and onion in a skillet until cooked through.
- To the cooked beef and onion, add rice, salt, pepper, garlic salt and 1 c tomato sauce and heat until warm.
- Fill each bell pepper with the beef/rice mixture.
- Pour remaining tomato sauce over the stuffed pepper, cover with lid or aluminum foil and bake for 40 minutes.
- Remove cover, sprinkle with mozzarella cheese and bake for an additional 10 minutes. Serve!

MEATBALLS

My "children" love these meatballs. Some of these "30 somethings" have been eating these out of my kitchen since their elementary and middle school years, and I have had numerous calls over the years asking "Ms. Karen, can you tell me how to make your meatballs?" Well, I have to confess that I have stood on the shoulders of giants. This recipe has been modified over the years, but it has been essentially sourced from a 30 year old cookbook that is now falling apart. MY cooking bible.

❖ Ingredients:

- Ground Beef - 1 lb (80/20 for this)
- Dry Bread Crumbs - 1/2 c
- Milk - 1/4 c
- Onion - 1/4 c fine diced
- Egg - 1
- Salt - 1/2 tsp
- Pepper - 1/4 tsp
- Worcestershire Sauce - 1 tsp
- Fresh Parsley - 1/4 c

❖ Tools:

- Large Glass Baking Dish
- Mixing Bowl and Spatula
- Sharp Knife
- Cutting Board
- Measuring Cups and Spoons
- Tongs

❖ Directions:

- Preheat oven to 400 degrees.
- Finely chop the onion and the parsley - you will need approximately 1/4 cup of each.
- Place the ground beef, egg, Worcestershire Sauce, milk, onion and parsley in your mixing bowl and work it with CLEAN hands until the ingredients are thoroughly blended.
- Add the bread crumbs, salt and pepper and hand blend again.
- Roll into 2" balls and place in an ungreased baking dish with the sides touching. Bake for 20-30 minutes or until your "I just need to see if they are done" taste testing sample is brown through.

Serving Suggestion: Sauce these babies up and eat them with a side of mashed potatoes or put them on a pasta noodle that will stand up to the heartiness of the meatballs. You can always just eat them straight out of the baking dish!

MEATLOAF

My sweet baby (the older one) HATES meatloaf, but this is a dish that I grew up on and I LOVE it. If I was ever going to get to have this at home, I had to try to find ways to make it palatable for my guy, and this is why you see the Barbecue Sauce substitution suggestion. While he WILL NOT eat it with either ketchup or tomato sauce, he will totally eat it "barbecued". If you have a picky eater, try this version and see if you can make a meatloaf lover out of 'em.

❖ Ingredients:

- Ground Beef - 1 1/2 lb (80/20 for this)
- White Bread - 3 Slices
- Milk - 1 c
- Onion - 1/2 c fine diced
- Egg - 1
- Salt - 3/4 tsp
- Pepper - 1/4 tsp
- Worcestershire Sauce - 1 tbl
- Dry Mustard - 1/2 tsp
- Garlic Salt - 1/4 tsp
- Ketchup (or BBQ Sauce) - 1 c

❖ Tools:

- Large Glass Loaf Pan
- Mixing Bowl and Spoon
- Sharp Knife
- Cutting Board
- Measuring Cups and Spoons

❖ Directions:

- Preheat oven to 350 degrees.
- Finely chop the onion.
- Tear the bread into small fluffy pieces.
- Place all ingredients except the Ketchup (or BBQ Sauce) in your mixing bowl and work it with CLEAN hands until the ingredients are thoroughly blended.
- Form into a loaf and place in an ungreased loaf pan.
- Pour the Ketchup (or BBQ Sauce) over the entire loaf and bake for 1 /14 hours (or until brown through ... sampling may be required ;)

Serving Suggestion: Day 1 - Serve with a side of mashed potato and a family favorite second vegetable. Day 2 - Slice that cold meatloaf up and put it between two pieces of white bread with a little more Ketchup or BBQ Sauce and make a sandwich out of it!

"QUICK" LASAGNA

This is not a recipe that I ate very often as a child but it IS something that my baby's daddy and I ate quite a lot of in our early years. In fact, there were a number of pasta based dishes that we ate (fettuccine, cannelloni, spaghetti, etc) before carbs became a bad word. If funds are short, pasta was a good, inexpensive "go to". I would normally prepare my own sauce but this is my "make it quick" recipe. Hope you love it!

❖ Ingredients:

- Ground Beef - 1 lb
- Ricotta Cheese - 15 oz
- Mozzarella Cheese - 4 c
- Parmesan cheese - 1/2 c
- Your favorite Italian Sauce - 24 oz (I like Prego Three Cheese)
- Egg - 1
- Oven-Ready Lasagna Noodles - 1 box
- Garlic Salt - 1/2 tsp

❖ Tools:

- Glass Baking Dish
- Skillet
- Mixing Bowl
- Mixing Spoon
- Measuring Cups and Spoons

❖ Directions:

- Preheat oven to 375 degrees.
- Brown ground beef over medium low heat. Drain liquid (fat) and add Italian sauce. Turn down heat to simmer.
- Combine ricotta, egg, 2 c mozzarella, 1/4 c parmesan and 1/2 tsp garlic salt and mix thoroughly.
- Spray baking dish with non-stick spray. Place lasagna noodle sheets side by side (they should touch but not overlap) and cover with sauce, ricotta cheese mixture, and mozzarella in that order until you reach the top of your baking dish (you should finish with mozzarella).
- Top it all off with a sprinkle of the remaining parmesan, cover with aluminum foil, place on a baking sheet (to catch the drippings) and bake for 25-30 minutes.
- Remove foil and bake an additional 10 minutes. Finish with 3-5 minutes under the broiler. Remove from the oven and allow to rest for 10-15 minutes.
- Cut into generous rectangles and serve with some garlic bread and a nice salad.

POT ROAST AND DAY 2 HASH

I love all of the possibilities that come with a Pot Roast. Talk about a dish that can be stretched! I can make it the traditional way, which lends itself easily to a Day 2 meal plan, or I can change up the vegetables to accommodate individual likes and dislikes. The recipe below is my favorite because it can be transformed into a Day 2 meal that I love (and enjoyed quite a lot growing up), but you should feel free to modify to your family's preferences.

❖ Day 1 Meal:

- Ingredients - 4 lb Beef Pot Roast, 1 tsp Salt, 1/2 tsp Pepper, 1 tsp Thyme, 1/2 tsp Oregano, 1 c Beef Broth, 3 lrg Carrots, 2 lrg Potatoes, 1 lrg Onion, 2 stalks Celery, 2 cloves Garlic, 1 tbl Canola Oil
- Tools - Dutch Oven, Sharp Knife, Cutting Board
- Directions: Preheat oven to 325 degrees. Wash, peel and cut carrots and potatoes into 1-2" chunks. Wash and cut celery into 1" pieces. Peel and cut onion into quarters. Peel garlic and leave whole. Cover all sides of the pot roast with salt and pepper and press into the meat. Heat the canola oil in the dutch oven over medium heat. Brown the pot roast on all sides and remove from the heat. Add the vegetables, oregano and thyme and pour in beef broth. Cover and bake for 3- 3 1/2 hours or until the beef pulls apart easily with a fork.
- Serving Suggestions: Serve directly from the dutch oven.

❖ Day 2 Meal:

- Ingredients - Left Overs from Day 1 Pot Roast, sliced White Bread (or Cornbread), Salt and Pepper
- Tools - Large Skillet (I prefer my cast iron), Sharp Knife, Cutting Board
- Directions: Cut up left over pot roast and vegetables into small dice and place in skillet. Add 1/4 - 1 cup of water (depending on the amount of hash that results from your left overs). You want some gravy so you will have to "eyeball" this. Heat over medium heat until warm through. If it ends up being too soupy, cook it until some of the water evaporates. Salt and pepper to taste.
- Serving Suggestions: Serve directly over White bread or cornbread.

RED BEANS AND RICE

DO NOT let the list of ingredients scare you away from this dish. It is worth the effort. Serve it with your favorite baked bread!

❖ Ingredients:

- Red Beans - 2 16 oz Cans
- Roasted Tomatoes - 1 Can
- Red Onion - 1 Medium
- Garlic - 1 Clove
- Bacon - 3 Slices
- Green (Bell) Pepper - 1 Medium
- Celery - 1 stalk
- Rice - 1 c uncooked
  (Not the Quick Cook kind)
- Chicken Stock - 2 1/2 c
- Onion Powder - 1 tsp
- Salt - 1 1/2 teaspoon
- Olive Oil
- Hot Sauce - 1/2 tsp (optional)
- Cilantro (optional)

❖ Tools:

- Large Pot
- Sauté Pan
- Cutting Board
- Sharp Knife
- Spatula

❖ Directions:

- Dice your onion, celery and green peppers. Peel and mince your garlic.
- Cut the bacon into 1/2" pieces.
- Heat 1 tbl olive oil over medium to medium-high heat in a saucepan/skillet. Add your bacon, minced garlic, diced onion, celery and green pepper and sauté until tender.
- Add your drained and rinsed red beans, onion powder, salt and hot sauce and stir to blend. Reduce heat to low and let simmer for 20 minutes.
- Bring chicken stock to a boil in your pot. Stir in the rice, return to a boil, reduce heat to low, cover and cook until tender (around 15-20 minutes).
- Mix the rice and beans mixture together and transfer to serving dishes.
- Top with chopped cilantro and serve.

RED BEANS AND RICE V2

(AUNT NANCY'S VERSION)

Aunt Nancy was full of love and life! I do not have a single memory of her without a smile on her lips and her arms open to hug me. It may be that everything tasted better only because she made it and I loved her. The only way for you to find out is to make it for yourself!

❖ Ingredients:

- Ground Beef - 1 lb
- Salt - 2 teaspoons
- Chili Powder - 1 teaspoon
- Onion - 1 Large
- Tomatoes - 1 c
- Water - 1 c
- Minute Rice - 1 1/2 c uncooked
- Kidney Beans - 1 Can
- Minced Garlic - 1 teaspoon (optional)

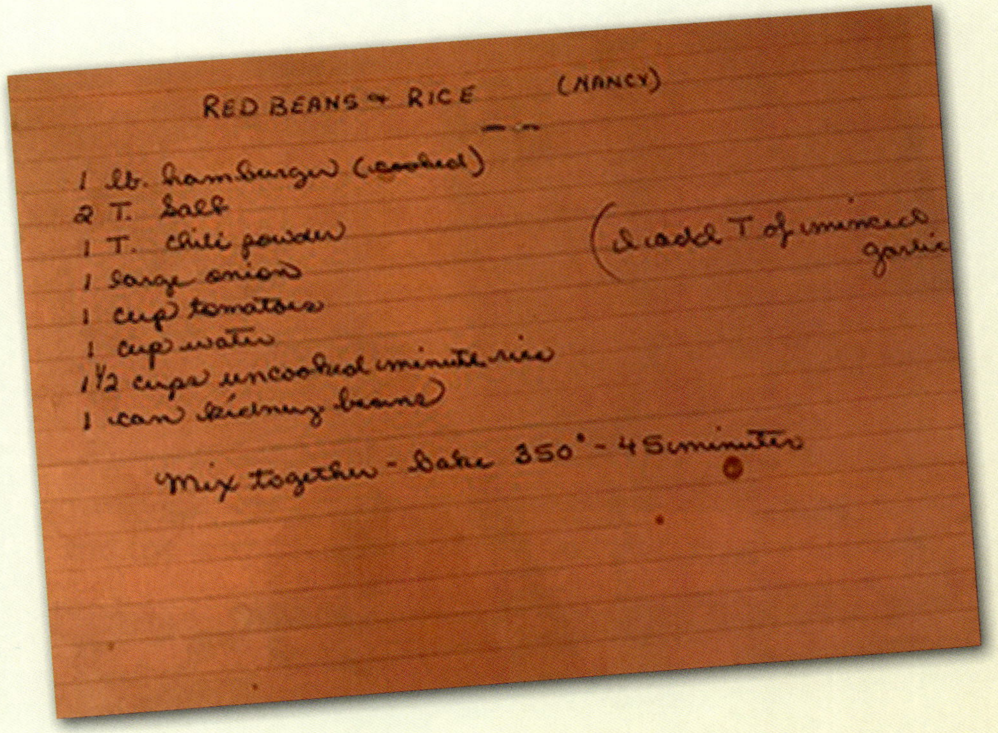

❖ Directions:

- Preheat oven to 350 degrees.
- Cook and drain ground beef.
- Chop onion and tomatoes into chunks.
- Mix all ingredients thoroughly in a large baking dish and bake for 45 minutes.

Veggies

BAKED BEANS

This is obviously going to be a very simple recipe and I am using canned goods so there is very little prep. To remind you, this is one of those recipes that is not going to give explicit measurements. This is a very personalized version (sweet and tangy) and you should takes steps to modify the recipe to your tastes.

❖ Ingredients:

- Canned Baked Beans (I love Bush's)
- Onion
- Yellow mustard
- Bacon

❖ Tools:

- Baking Dish
- Sharp Knife

❖ Directions:

- Preheat oven to 375 degrees.
- Open the cans of baked beans and pour into the baking dish.
- Dice the onion and add to the beans.
- Add yellow mustard and combine all ingredients.
- Lay 3 pieces of bacon on top and bake for 30-45 minutes (until bubbly).

BRUSSELS SPROUTS

This is another very simple recipe using very few ingredients. Brussels sprouts are one of my favorite vegetables. You can steam them, bake them or, as in this case, fry them up! When in doubt, a Southerner always throws that s&@t in a skillet!

❖ Ingredients:

- A bunch of fresh Brussels Sprouts
- 6 slices of Hickory Smoked Bacon
- Shallots (or Onion)
- Salt and Pepper

❖ Tools:

- Iron Skillet with Lid
- Sharp Knife
- Cutting Board
- Colander

❖ Directions:

- Wash the brussels sprouts, trim off the stalk end, remove outside leaves and halve.
- Slice bacon in 1/2" pieces.
- Dice shallot.
- Add bacon to the skillet and begin to cook, making sure to separate the pieces as much as possible.
- After the bacon starts to curl up and the fat begins to render, add the diced shallot and halved brussels sprouts. Cook to desired level of doneness (I like mine a little charred).
- Plate and enjoy!

CORNBREAD DRESSING

My Mom is famous for this cornbread dressing. It is a meal all by itself and is wonderful as leftovers. It takes a little work (as most things do) but is worth the effort. Because it takes some knife work and the cooking and cooling of some elements, it is best prepared the day before you need it.

❖ Ingredients:

- Large Skillet of Cornbread
- Chicken - 1 lrg boneless breast
- Celery - 5 stalks
- Onion - 1 lrg
- Fresh Parsley - 1/3 c
- Chicken Broth - 4-5 c
- Sage - to taste
- Poultry Seasoning - to taste
- Salt and Pepper

❖ Tools:

- Sauce Pan
- Sharp Knife
- Cutting Board
- Large Baking Dish

❖ Directions:

- Boil the chicken breast until done through. Cool and pull into small pieces.
- Dice celery and onion. Chop parsley.
- Using a little olive oil, sauté the celery, onion and parsley until the onion is translucent.
- Crumble up the cornbread.
- Mix all ingredients in your baking dish (it should be soupy). Season and taste, season and taste, season and taste. I like mine sage heavy but you should make it your own.
- Bake in a 350 degree oven for 1 hour or until the top begins to brown and the dressing is no longer soupy. Now enjoy today and then enjoy tomorrow!

FRIED CORN

Now, if you were raised north of the Mason-Dixon Line or West of the Mississippi River, then you might think that this is literally deep fried corn, but this is actually something a little different. Remember when I told you to keep your left over bacon grease? Well, you are going to be using some of that in this recipe. I remember many summer days spent shucking and cutting corn with great fondness, and this is a versatile dish I love.

❖ Ingredients:

- Corn (White or Yellow) - 12 Ears
- Sugar - 2 tbl
- Bacon Grease - 2 tbl
- Salt - 1/2 tsp
- Pepper - 1/4 tsp
- Butter - 2 tbl
- Water - 1/2-1 c

❖ Tools:

- Large Mixing Bowl
- Sharp Knife
- Skillet with Lid
- Spatula
- Butter Knife

❖ Directions:

- Shuck and clean the silk from the corn.
- Wash and dry the corn (still on the cob).
- Turning the cob upside down and holding firmly with the end of the stalk, cut the corn from the cob with downward slices of a sharp knife (only the top half of each kernel).
- Using the back side of a butter knife, you should firmly drag it down the cob to remove the "cream" from the remaining kernels.
- Heat 2 tbl bacon grease in the skillet over medium low heat.
- When melted, add the corn and "cream" to the skillet along with the sugar, salt and pepper and 3/4 c water (it should be a little soupy).
- Bring to a boil. Reduce heat to low, cover and cook for 30 minutes.
- Remove lid and cook until the water cooks off. Add butter and serve!

❖ Variation:

- If you like things spicy, trying adding a little diced jalapeño!

CORN CASSEROLE

This is a dish that I made for a family Thanksgiving Dinner, and it was the only empty dish left after the dinner portion of Thanksgiving was over! There were actually grumbles about there being none left to include in their "take home" dishes. That made me smile! So, if you want a dish that literally pleased everyone... here you go! Note: This is an exceptionally large dish that will serve a small army.

❖ Ingredients:

- Butter - 1 c (2 sticks)
- Eggs - 4 large
- Packaged Dry Cornbread Mix - 2 8.5 oz pkgs
- Canned Whole Kernel Corn - 2 15 oz cans
- Canned Creamed Corn - 2 14.75 oz cans
- Sour Cream - 2 cups

❖ Tools:

- 18 x 9 Baking Dish
- Medium Mixing Bowl
- Mixing Spatula

❖ Directions:

- Preheat oven to 375 degrees.
- Lightly butter your baking dish.
- Lightly beat eggs until just blended.
- Melt Butter.
- Blend together all ingredients in a medium mixing bowl.
- Pour mixture into your buttered baking dish and bake for 45 minutes to 1 hour or until browned.

FRIED GREEN TOMATOES

We wait all year for the tomato season to start so that we can harvest green tomatoes for our dinner table. Funny enough, these are prepared very similarly to fried chicken. You can get very creative with these so be prepared to amend the recipe to your tastes.

❖ Ingredients:

- Green Tomatoes - 3 medium
- Eggs - 3
- Flour - 1 c
- Cornmeal - 1/4 c
- Salt and Pepper
- (optional) Paprika and Garlic Salt to taste
- Vegetable Oil

❖ Tools:

- Medium Bowl
- Whisk
- Skillet (cast iron is best)
- Paper Towels

❖ Directions:

- Slice your cleaned tomatoes to 1/4" slices.
- In a shallow bowl, beat eggs. In a separate shallow bowl (or plate), blend your dry ingredients thoroughly. Be sure to taste test your dry mix and add seasoning to your tastes.
- Heat 4-5 tbl of oil in skillet over medium low heat until hot but not smoking.
- While the skillet is heating, begin preparing your tomato slices. Begin by dipping the slices in the egg and then covering them with the dry mix and REPEAT. Each slice should go through the egg and dry mix twice.
- The slices then go straight into the heated skillet. Cook each side until crispy (3-5 minutes) and remove to paper towels to help remove some of the oil.
- Serve immediately.

Serving Suggestion: These are delish served unadorned, but I also serve mine with hot sauce, ketchup, Ranch Dressing, or a mix of a strong mustard and mayo.

FRIED OKRA

I have a story about this one. When I was young, I HATED okra with a passion. My brother hated squash. If mom made one for dinner (vegetable...not child) she inevitably would fix the other. The rule in the house at the time was that you could not leave the table until your plate was clean. Sooo, Rick and I would just wait until mom's back was turned and then we would eat off each other's plates. Proof positive that we COULD get along when we were both motivated to!

❖ Ingredients:

- Okra - 2 lb (fresh from the garden if possible)
- Eggs - 3 large
- Milk - 1/2 c
- Cornmeal - 1/2 c
- Flour - 1 c
- Salt - 1 tsp
- Pepper - 1/2 tsp
- Paprika - 1/2 tsp

❖ Tools:

- Large and Small Mixing Bowls
- Sharp Knife
- Cutting Board
- Large Skillet
- Measuring Cups and Spoons

❖ Directions:

- Clean okra. Cut off tops and tips. Cut the trunks into 1/2" pieces and put in the large mixing bowl.
- In the small bowl, beat eggs and milk together until just blended.
- Mix together the dry ingredients in a gallon size plastic bag.
- Pour the egg mixture over the okra and mix until the okra is coated well.
- Add the egg coated okra to the plastic bag in batches by the handful and then shake that thing like no tomorrow. Remove the coated okra to a plate and repeat the process until all the okra is coated with the dry mixture.
- Heat 1/2 c vegetable oil in your frying pan over medium heat and (after the oil is hot) fry the okra until they are crispy. You may have to do this in batches as well since you will want to fry them in a single layer.

GREEN BEANS

Now, I have prepared green beans two different ways for years. One way is definitely more healthy than the other, and one way is definitely more tasty. I will let you decide which suits you.

Tasty Green Beans

❖ Ingredients:

- 1 lb fresh Green Beans (or two large cans Cut Green Beans), Salt, Pepper, 4 Slices Smoked Bacon

❖ Tools:

- Medium Sauce Pan with Lid, Colander

❖ Directions:

- If using fresh green beans, put them in a colander and clean thoroughly. Discard water, snap off and discard ends and snap the remaining green bean in half. Place the snapped beans in the pan, add 1 c water (or just dump your canned green beans water and all into the pan), 4 slices of bacon and salt and pepper to taste. Bring to a boil, reduce heat to simmer, cover and allow to cook for at least 1 hour. Check seasoning and serve.

Healthy Green Beans

❖ Ingredients:

- 1 lb fresh Green Beans, Salt, Pepper, 4 Slices Smoked Bacon (optional)

❖ Tools:

- Medium Sauce Pan with Steamer Insert and Lid, Colander

❖ Directions:

- Place the green beans in a colander and clean thoroughly. Discard water, snap off and discard ends and snap the remaining green bean in half. Fill the pan to the half way mark with water and bring to a boil, add green beans (and bacon if you like) to the steamer insert and place into the pan of boiling water (water should not be touching the steamer insert). Cover and steam for 12-18 minutes (or until your desired doneness). Season with salt and pepper and serve.

MACARONI AND CHEESE

There is nothing to be said about Macaroni and Cheese that you do not already know. It is delicious, it is versatile and it can be eaten as a stand alone meal. What could be better?

❖ Ingredients:

- Elbow Macaroni - 4 c dried
- Sharp Cheddar Cheese - 1 lb (shredded)
- Butter - 1 stick + 2 tbl
- Egg - 1 lrg
- Milk - 2 1/2 c
- Flour - 1/4 c
- Dried Mustard - 3 tsp
- Salt - 1/2 tsp
- Pepper - 1/2 tsp
- Bread Crumbs - 1 c

❖ Tools:

- Large and Medium Pots/Saucepan
- Large Baking Dish
- Colander
- Measuring Cups and Spoons
- Whisk

❖ Directions:

- Preheat the oven to 350 degrees.
- Cook the macaroni in a large pot according to the directions on the packaging. DO NOT overcook. When done, dump into the colander and rinse with cool water.
- Beat the egg in a 1 c measuring cup.
- Melt 1 stick of butter in the medium saucepan over low heat. When it is fully melted, start whisking your flour in slowly. When it is smooth and bubbly, start whisking in your milk slowly. Add the mustard and continue to whisk until smooth.
- Remove from the heat and pour 1/4 c of the sauce into the beaten egg whisking constantly to prevent the egg cooking. Pour the egg mixture back into the sauce and blend. Add the cheese stirring again until the cheese has melted. Add salt and pepper and mix well.
- Put the drained macaroni in a buttered baking dish. Pour the sauce over the top and mix gently (make sure the macaroni is all coated). Top with a sprinkle of your favorite bread crumbs and bake for 30 minutes or until bubbly and brown on top.
- I can feel my hips growing and I JUST DON'T CARE!!!

TOMATO-FENNEL PASTA

This is one of the best pasta dishes that I have ever put in my mouth. AND, I make mine with Beyond Meat Hot Italian Sausage so it is healthier than it would be with other meats. Try this version. I know you are going to LOVE it even if it IS on the healthier side of things.

❖ Ingredients:

- Beyond Meat Italian Sausage - 1 pkg
- Olive Oil - 2 tbl
- Yellow Onion - 1 medium
- Garlic - 3 cloves
- Roasted Diced Tomatoes - 15 oz can
- Tomato Sauce - 15 oz can
- Salt - 1/2 tsp
- Sugar - 2 tsp
- Dried Parsley - 1 tbl
- Dried Basil - 1 tsp
- Dried Oregano - 1 tsp
- Fennel Seed - 1 tbl
- Bay Leaf - 1
- Penne Pasta - 15 oz

❖ Tools:

- Large Stock Pot
- Sharp Knife
- Cutting Board
- Measuring Cups and Spoons
- Large Pot for Pasta

❖ Directions:

- Dice the onion and peel and mince the garlic.
- Put the sausages in a dry, large stock pot and cook over medium-low heat until seared on all sides and heated through. Remove to a plate.
- Add the olive oil to the stock pot along with the diced onion and minced garlic. Sauté over medium-low heat until fragrant and the onions are translucent.
- Add the diced tomato and tomato sauce along with 1/2 c water to the stock pot along with the dry ingredients and bay leaf. Mix together, return sausages to the sauce and simmer over low heat (stirring occasionally) for 2 hours.
- Heat a large pot of salted water to a boil. Add pasta and cook to your desired level of doneness and then drain. DO NOT over cook as it will continue to cook after removed from the water.
- Remove sausages, cut into bite size pieces and return to the sauce along with the drained pasta. Heat over low for 15 to 20 minutes.

MASHED POTATOES

Mashed potatoes can be a side dish, an adornment or the component to a dish. They are SO very versatile. This recipe is the result of a hodge-podge of efforts on my part to make the very best mashed 'taters. Try them on their own, as a topping to Shepherd's Pie, or to make Potato Cakes!

❖ Ingredients:

- Potatoes - 4 large Russet
- Butter - 1 stick
- Half & Half - 1/2 to 1 1/2 c
- Salt and Pepper - to taste

❖ Tools:

- Peeler
- Large Pot
- Hand Mixer or Masher
- Measuring Cup
- Cutting Board
- Colander

❖ Directions:

- Wash and peel potatoes.
- Cut peeled potatoes into 2" chunks.
- Add potatoes to pot, cover with water, add 1 tsp salt and boil over medium-high heat until fork tender.
- Pour into colander to drain and then return the potatoes to the pot.
- Chunk the butter and add it to the pot along with 1 tsp salt and 1/2 tsp pepper. Move it around until the butter melts.
- Add the Half & Half to the pot 1/2 cup at a time, mashing (or mixing) in between until you come to the perfect consistency for YOU!

POTATO CAKES (DAY 2 DISH)

Okay. If you are not familiar with Potato Cakes, these might not sound appealing but they are really delicious and can be either a side dish or an entree. A nice bonus is that they are a "second day dish" meaning that they are a good use of left over mashed potatoes. In my family, we intentionally make extra mashed potatoes so that we can have potato cakes day 2.

❖ Ingredients:

- Leftover Mashed Potatoes - 3 cups
- Eggs - 2 lrg
- Flour - 1/2 c
- Salt
- Pepper
- Small Diced Onion (optional) - 1/4 c
- Vegetable Oil

❖ Tools:

- Medium Bowl
- Whisk
- Skillet (cast iron is best)
- Paper Towels

❖ Directions:

- Mix together cold mashed potato, eggs, flour, salt and pepper (and onion if desired) until smooth.
- Heat 3-4 tbl of oil in skillet over medium low heat until hot but not smoking and drop large spoonfuls of potato mixture into skillet, flattening them a little to make a pancake shape.
- Cook each side until crispy (2-3 minutes) and remove to paper towels to help remove some of the oil.
- Serve immediately or chill to serve cold.

Serving Suggestion: These can be served as a main with a side of applesauce and are DELICIOUS, as a side dish for almost anything (but are especially good with a Brat), or cold as a snack.

POTATO CASSEROLES

There are about as many recipes for potato casserole as there are whiskeys my husband likes. The ones that I am sharing with you here are just the ones that I learned over the years from family and friends. I hope there is one here that you will enjoy.

Option 1

❖ Ingredients:

- 1 pkg frozen Shredded Potato (frozen is best I have found in this case), 1 can Cream of Mushroom Soup, 1 small Onion, 1 - 1 1/2 c Milk, 2 c Shredded Cheddar Cheese, Salt and Pepper

❖ Tools:

- Sharp Knife, 1 1/2 qt Baking Dish, Large Mixing Bowl and Mixing Spoon

❖ Directions:

- Preheat oven to 375 degrees. Butter the bottom of the casserole dish. Small dice the onion. Add all of the ingredients to the mixing bowl and blend thoroughly (it should be a little soupy). Transfer to your casserole dish and bake uncovered for 30-45 minutes or until you have a crunchy top. Remove from the oven and allow to rest for 15 minutes prior to serving.

Option 2

❖ Ingredients:

- 3 medium Potatoes, 1 medium Onion, 1 Green Bell Pepper, 1 Red Bell Pepper, Salt, Pepper, Milk, 1 stick Butter, Small Block Cheddar Cheese

❖ Tools:

- Sharp Knife, Peeler, 2 qt Baking Dish, Aluminum Foil

❖ Directions:

- Preheat oven to 325 degrees. Butter the bottom and sides of the casserole dish. Peel and slice potatoes into rounds. Peel and slice onion into thin slices. Clean bell peppers, slice in half and remove seeds and membranes. Slice further into 1/4" slices. Cut cheese into 1/4" cubes. Cut butter into 1/2 tablespoon slices. In the baking dish, layer potato, onion, bell peppers, salt and pepper and cheese in as many layers as you can. Top with pats of butter and pour milk over the entire casserole until it reaches the top layer. Cover tightly with aluminum foil and bake for 1 1/2 hours. Remove aluminum foil and bake uncovered until the top is browned.

TWICE BAKED POTATOES

These are so tasty that they sometimes refuse to accept second billing on any dinner plate. Also, they are remarkably good day two with a little reheat in the oven or a quick zap in the microwave (although this can diminish the crispiness of the potato skin... if this is important to you)!

❖ Ingredients:

- Baking Potato - 2 lrg
- Bacon - 6 slices
- Cheddar Cheese - 1 1/2 c
- Sour Cream - 4 oz
- Butter - 4 tbl
- Salt - 1/2 tsp
- Pepper - 1/4 tsp
- Jalapeño (optional)

❖ Tools:

- Sharp Knife
- Large Spoon
- Skillet
- Chopping Board
- Mixing Bowl
- Cookie Sheet

❖ Directions:

- Wash, dry and bake potatoes at 475 degrees for approximately 45 minutes or until a fork goes in easily.
- Cook bacon until crispy. Remove to a paper towel to cool.
- Let baked potatoes cool for 15 minutes.
- Halve the potatoes lengthwise (be careful not to tear the skins).
- Scoop the potato out and into the mixing bowl, leaving the potato skins looking like little canoes.
- Mix the warm potato with the sour cream, butter, salt, pepper, 3/4 of the cheddar cheese and the optional chopped jalapeño. Fill potato skins with the mixture and top with crumbled bacon and the remaining cheese.
- Bake on a cookie sheet at 375 degrees for 30 minutes and ENJOY!

SKILLET SQUASH

Now, THIS is one of MY favorite side dishes. I top mine with shredded cheddar cheese and LOVE it. My brother on the other hand has had to learn to LIKE it. When we were young, we were not allowed to leave the table until our plates were clean. Sometimes this was easy and sometimes it required a little bit of sibling cooperation. True story. My brother HATED squash and I HATED okra. Invariably, mom would serve both at a meal and we would end up sitting at the table long after everyone else had left. While mom was cleaning the kitchen (with her back turned), Rick and I would eat off each other's plates until all the offending vegetables were gone. This little subterfuge went on for years with mom feeling triumphant at getting us to eat things we professed to hate and us feeling triumphant at having pulled one over on her (not an easy task). LOL

❖ Ingredients:

- Bacon Grease - 3 tbl
- Yellow Squash - 3 medium
- Onion - 1 large
- Water - 3/4 c
- Salt and Pepper
- Shredded Cheddar Cheese (Optional)
- Buttered Bread Crumbs (Optional)

❖ Tools:

- Large Skillet
- Spatula
- Sharp Knife
- Cutting Board

❖ Directions:

- Slice the onion and squash to 1/8" rounds (or thicker if you like).
- Melt bacon grease over medium-low heat in the skillet.
- Add squash, onion, salt, pepper and water to the skillet.
- Turn the heat up to medium and allow to cook until the squash begins to break down and the water has mostly evaporated (note: you may need to add additional water).
- When done you can either serve directly from the skillet or transfer to a buttered baking dish, top with cheese and buttered bread crumbs and bake until you have a crunchy top.

STEWED TOMATOES

This is one of the simplest recipes you are ever going to find. It is simply done and is one of my love duck's favorites.

❖ Ingredients:

- 2 cans of diced tomatoes, 3 tbl butter, 6-8 slices of white bread, salt, pepper and sugar (to taste)

❖ Tools:

- Large Skillet, Spatula

❖ Directions:

- Melt butter over medium-low heat in the skillet, add canned tomatoes and cook until the tomatoes begin to break down.
- Add salt, pepper and sugar (to taste), reduce heat to simmer and allow to cook for 5 minutes.
- Tear bread into small pieces and add to the skillet. Stir until the bread is completely incorporated into the tomatoes. Serve. THAT'S ALL THERE IS TO IT!

❖ Alternate Directions:

- Honestly, if you're in a hurry, you can just throw everything in the skillet at once! (pictured here)

SWEET POTATO CASSEROLE

The choice of which Sweet Potato Casserole to serve for Thanksgiving dinner can start a full on war in our house. I am providing you with both versions. You will have to decide for yourself what will appeal to you and yours. To avoid whining and accusations of favoritism, I encourage you to warn dinner attendees in advance about the preparation you will present. If they do not like your choice, tell them that they are welcome to bring their own along with an extra bottle of wine for the cook.

Option 1

❖ Ingredients:

- 6 medium Sweet Potatoes, 3/4 c Brown Sugar, 1 tsp Salt, 1/4 c Butter +, 1 c Mini Marshmallows

❖ Tools:

- Butter Knife, Sharp Knife, Peeler, 1 1/2 qt Baking Dish

❖ Directions:

- Preheat oven to 375 degrees. Butter the bottom of the casserole dish. Peel and slice sweet potatoes to 1/4" slices. Mix brown sugar and salt. Layer the ingredients (potato, sprinkle of brown sugar/salt, pats of butter) until all are used. Finish with the brown sugar/salt mix. Bake uncovered for 30 minutes or until a fork goes through the potatoes easily. Sprinkle mini marshmallows over the top and then bake for another 5-10 minutes (until marshmallows begin to brown).

Option 2

❖ Ingredients:

- 4 medium Sweet Potatoes (3 cups mashed), 1 c Sugar, 1 c Brown Sugar, 1/2 c Butter melted + 1/4 c more cut into small pats, 1 tsp Vanilla Extract, 2 eggs slightly beaten, 1 c chopped Pecans, 1/3 c All Purpose Flour

❖ Tools:

- Butter Knife, Sharp Knife, Peeler, 1 1/2 qt Baking Dish

❖ Directions:

- Preheat over to 350 degrees. Butter the bottom and sides of the casserole dish. Peel and cut sweet potatoes into large chunks and boil until soft. Drain and mash. Mix mashed sweet potatoes with sugar, 1/2 c melted butter, vanilla and slightly beaten eggs. Turn into buttered casserole dish. Mix brown sugar, flour, butter and pecans and sprinkle over the top. Bake uncovered for 45 minutes.

TURNIP/COLLARD GREENS

Another (much maligned) yummy vegetable! We love our greens, and fresh picked out of the garden is the best. That canned stuff just will not do after you have had fresh greens. The key here is to remember that it takes A LOT of fresh greens to make a serving of cooked greens, but you want to do it. I promise.

❖ Ingredients:

- Turnip / Collard Greens - 2 large bundles (about 1 lb.)
- Bacon - 6 thick cut slices
- Salt
- Pepper
- Liquid Smoke (optional)

❖ Tools:

- Large Pot

❖ Directions:

- Wash the greens thoroughly.
- Judiciously trim off the tough part of the stems.
- Tear the leaves into large pieces and put them in the pot.
- Season with salt and pepper, top with uncooked bacon, cover with water (and a few drops of liquid smoke if desired) and bring to a boil.
- Once the water begins to boil, reduce heat to simmer, cover and cook for 50 minutes or until tender.

Note: That juice left after cooking greens is called "Pot Likker," and it is a yummy soup base, so don't throw that stuff away!

Soups & Sandwiches

CHICKEN NOODLE SOUP

Chicken Noodle Soup is my "I don't feel good" soup. There is just something about this combination of broth, veggies, chicken and noodles that makes us feel better. An additional perk is that it is a really simple dish to prepare with only a little knife work and left over plain boiled chicken (okay, well maybe not but the chef gets to decide how much and if I say there is extra chicken, then there is extra chicken) to munch on if you are wanting something really bland but filling.

❖ Ingredients:

- Olive Oil - 1 tbl
- Onion - 1/2 large
- Celery - 2 large stalks
- Carrots - 4 small
- Chicken Bone Broth - 32 oz
- Better Than Bouillon Roasted Chicken Base - 2 tbl
- Wide Egg Noodles - 6 oz (1/2 pkg)
- Chicken Breasts - 2 boneless skinless
- Salt and Pepper (to taste)

❖ Tools:

- Sharp Knife
- Cutting Board
- Spatula
- Ladle
- Large Soup Pan with Lid
- Medium Pan

❖ Directions:

- Fill medium pan half full of water, add the chicken and bring to a boil. Reduce heat and allow to simmer until chicken is done through (8-12 minutes based on chicken size).
- While your chicken is cooking, peel and small dice your onion. Peel and medium dice your carrots and medium dice your celery.
- Add olive oil, onion, carrots, celery and salt and pepper (to taste) to the large soup pan and heat over medium to medium-low heat and cook/stir until onion is translucent.
- Slowly add your chicken bone broth and the Better Than Bouillon base and stir thoroughly. Add egg noodles and allow to simmer uncovered.
- At some point in this process, your chicken will be done. Remove it to a plate to cool (keep the cooking water). After it cools, pull it apart into small pieces.
- Now, check your broth. Taste it. Is it too salty? Add water (from cooking the chicken) until you get to your perfect saline level. After you reach YOUR perfect broth, add your chicken, stir, cover and remove from the heat. Allow it to sit for at least 15 minutes and serve! So good on a day where that tummy just will not settle down.

CHILI / CORN PONE PIE

Chili is a very controversial dish. My recipe kinda takes a "middle of the road" approach. It cannot be said enough. Make it yours. Play with the ingredients until you get YOUR perfect bowl of chili.

❖ Ingredients:

- Olive oil
- Onion - 1 medium
- Garlic - 2 cloves
- Ground Beef - 1 lb
- Roasted Diced Tomatoes - 2 cans
- Chili Beans - 2 cans
- Chili Powder - 1 tbl
- Cumin - 1 tbl
- Oregano - 1 tbl
- Salt - 1 tsp
- Pepper - 1/2 tsp
- Unsweetened Hershey's Chocolate Powder - 1 tsp
- Hot Sauce - 1-2 tsp

❖ Tools:

- Sharp Knife
- Cutting Board
- Spatula, Ladle
- Large Soup Pan (or Dutch Oven) with Lid

❖ Directions:

- Peel and small dice your onion. Mince your garlic.
- Add 2-3 tbl olive oil, onion, garlic and spices to your soup pan and heat over medium to medium-low heat until onion is translucent.
- Add your ground beef and cook through.
- Add your canned tomatoes, chili beans (with liquid) and hot sauce. Bring mixture to a boil, reduce heat to simmer and cover with a lid. Cook for 30-45 minutes to allow the flavors to meld.
- TASTE and adjust as necessary. Serve with crackers, Fritos, cheese, sour cream, jalapeños, etc. GO CRAZY!

Grandma Gayle's Variation on Chili: If you have a cast iron dutch oven, make your chili in the dutch oven and make it really, really soupy. Pour cornbread mix (see page 116) over the top and bake in the oven until the corn bread is done. Voilà! Grandma Gayle's Corn Pone Pie. This is yummy, yummy, yummy.

COUSIN WES'S WILD CHILI

Cousin Wes is a beautiful man inside and out. Imagine a beautiful, infectious smile found under a ball cap walking across an open field toting a rifle and you can see our cousin. He and his brother, Lee, hunt and the products of their hunts are processed and eaten. What you find below is one end product of a successful hunting season. Now, I respect this but I was the farm girl who had to leave the property when the pigs / cows were slaughtered. I eat meat but I always pretend that I DO NOT know where it came from!

❖ Ingredients:

- Ground Pork - 2 lbs
- Ground Turkey - 2 lbs
- Ground Deer - 2 lbs
- Northern Kidney Beans - 3 cans
- Pinto Beans - 3 cans
- Del Monte Oregano Basil Diced Tomatoes - 3 cans
- Water - fill one of the unrinsed tomato cans (we want all that tomatoey goodness!)
- McCormick Original Chili Seasoning - 6 packages
- Onion - 1 lrg
- Celery - 4 stalks
- Bell Pepper - 1 lrg
- Tomatoes - 8 medium
- Tomato Sauce - 2 cans
- Jalapeño
- Olive Oil

❖ Tools:

- Large Skillet
- Large Pot
- Sharp Knife
- Cutting Board
- Colander

❖ Directions:

- Dice onions, celery, jalapeño, tomatoes and bell pepper.
- Strain beans.
- Brown meat and strain out grease.
- Sauté vegetables in a little olive oil.
- Mix sautéed vegetables, browned meat, kidney and pinto beans, tomatoes, tomato sauce, McCormick Chili Seasoning Mix and water in a large pot and simmer over low heat for 45 minutes to an hour.
- Serve that up with some cornbread, crackers and / or Fritos and your favorite toppings.

POTATO SOUP

I LOVE Potato Soup. It is one of my favorite winter dishes. It has the additional perk of being relatively inexpensive to make (depending, of course, on how you serve it) and it is really versatile. You can make it chunky, smooth, top it with cheese, bacon, chives, eat it with crackers, croutons or bread or serve it as a side dish with a salad or sandwich. Regardless, it is super satisfying.

❖ Ingredients:

- Onion - 1 large
- Potatoes - 2 large
- Butter - 4 tbl
- Flour - 3 tbl
- Salt - 2 tsp
- Pepper - 1/4 tsp
- Chicken Broth - 4 c (I use bone broth)
- Heavy Cream - 3/4 c

❖ Tools:

- Sharp Knife
- Cutting Board
- Spatula
- Ladle
- Large Soup Pan with Lid
- Immersion Blender (optional)

❖ Directions:

- Peel and small dice your onion. Peel and large dice (1/2") your potato.
- Add butter and onion to your soup pan and heat over medium to medium-low heat for about a minute before adding the diced potato.
- Continue to cook until the onion is translucent and the potato has started to brown. Add your flour, salt and pepper and blend until you have a paste.
- Slowly add your chicken stock, stirring constantly.
- Bring mixture to a boil, reduce heat to simmer and cover with a lid.
- Cook for 30 minutes or until your potatoes are tender. TASTE and adjust as necessary.
- Remove from heat, add your heavy cream and either serve chunky or use your immersion blender to blend to your desired consistency. BE CAREFUL! Those immersion blenders have been known to spit hot liquid at you... nasty creatures but super helpful.

CREAMY PUMPKIN SOUP

You can find the most WONDERFUL recipes in the strangest places. The origin of this one is unknown but from the looks of it, it came through the mail as part of a nutrition flyer (although I obviously messed that up with my incessant need for butter and Half and Half :). It is really delicious on a cold winter day with some crusty bread AND BUTTER!

❖ Ingredients:

- Pumpkin - 3 c
- Carrots - 2 medium
- Celery - 3 stalks
- Onion - 1 medium
- Chicken Broth - 6 c
- Curry Powder - 1/2 tsp
- Cinnamon - 1/2 tsp
- Clove - 1/8 tsp
- Butter - 4 tbl
- Olive Oil - 2 tbl
- Half and Half - 1/2 c
- Salt and Pepper - to taste

❖ Tools:

- Large Sauce Pan
- Sharp Knife and Cutting Board
- Peeler or Paring Knife
- Measuring Spoons and Cup
- Blender or Immersion Blender

❖ Directions:

- Peel and chop onion, celery and carrot. Peel and chunk the fresh pumpkin.
- Add a little olive oil to the sauce pan and sauté the pumpkin until tender. Remove to a plate.
- Add olive oil and butter to the sauce pan and heat over medium low heat. Add the onion, carrot and celery and sauté until fragrant and tender (3-5 minutes).
- Return the pumpkin to the sauce pan along with the broth and spices. Bring to a boil and then reduce heat and simmer for 30 minutes.
- Purée the contents of the pan.
- Remove from heat and add the half and half and blend thoroughly.
- Salt and pepper to taste.

ROASTED RED PEPPER AND TOMATO SOUP

This soup is delicious on its own or partnered with a grilled cheese. It can be made more hardy by the addition of some cooked rice or pasta. This dish is begging for you to be creative!

❖ Ingredients:

- Fire Roasted Canned Diced Tomatoes - 28 oz can
- Roasted Red Peppers - 12 oz jar
- "Better Than Bouillon" Roasted Chicken Base - 2 tbl
- Sugar - 2 tbl
- Water - 1 c
- Butter - 4 tbl
- Half and Half - 1/2 c
- Salt and Pepper - to taste

❖ Tools:

- Large Sauce Pan
- Measuring Spoons and Cup
- Blender or Immersion Blender

❖ Directions:

- Empty canned roasted tomato and roasted red peppers into the large saucepan.
- Add bouillon, water and sugar and heat over medium low heat for 5-7 minutes or until hot.
- Remove from heat and add butter and half and half.
- Allow butter to melt and then either blend in a blender (or use an immersion blender) until smooth.
- Salt and pepper to taste.
- Return stove and simmer while you prepare your optional grilled cheese or rice/pasta!

CARROT-GINGER SOUP

Compliments of my bright and beautiful daughter! Enjoy!!

❖ Ingredients:

- Shallot - 1 medium
- Onion - 1/2 medium
- Ginger - 2" piece
- Carrot - 3 1/2 c chopped
- Olive Oil - 2 tbl
- Butter - 2 tbl
- Vegetable Broth - 4 c
- Orange Juice - 1/3 c
- Half and Half - 1/2 c
- Salt - 1 tsp
- Pepper - 1/4 tsp
- Parsley - 1/2 tsp
- Savory - Dash

❖ Tools:

- Large Sauce Pan
- Sharp Knife and Cutting Board
- Peeler or paring knife
- Measuring Spoons and Cup
- Blender or Immersion Blender

❖ Directions:

- Peel and chop shallot, onion, ginger and carrot.
- Add olive oil and butter to the sauce pan and heat over medium low heat.
- Add vegetables and sauté until fragrant and tender (3-5 minutes).
- Add orange juice and simmer for 5 minutes.
- Purée the contents of the pan and strain to remove any strings from the ginger.
- Pour back into the pan and add the vegetable broth and the seasonings. Allow to simmer for 30-45 minutes over low heat.
- Remove from heat and add the half and half.
- Blend in a blender (or use an immersion blender) until smooth.
- Salt and pepper to taste.
- Return stove and simmer while you prepare your optional grilled cheese or rice / pasta!

FRIED BOLOGNA SANDWICH

My youth was spent eating fried bologna sandwiches and then countering the cholesterol consumption with bowls of oatmeal. No joke, my family could find MANY ways to cook up bologna and make a meal out of it. Seriously, I think it was a precursor to Spam. Provided here is how we made my favorite sandwich!

❖ Ingredients:

- Sliced Bologna
- Cheese Slice Singles
- Mustard
- Mayo
- Fresh Tomato
- White Bread (why even make the gesture of trying to make this more healthy with Wheat Bread)
- Butter

❖ Tools:

- Skillet (I prefer non-stick for this)
- Spatula
- Sharp Knife

❖ Directions:

- Make 1" cuts in your bologna slices at 1:30, 4:30, 7;30 and 10:30 by the clock. It makes your bologna look a little like a Knights Templar cross and also minimizes the bowing when you fry it up.
- Thinly slice your clean tomato.
- If you are using a non-stick skillet, go ahead and throw the bologna in and heat the skillet to medium/medium-low heat. (If you are using a cast iron skillet, use a little cooking spray to prime that thing.) Fry the bologna until light brown on both sides and remove to a plate. Put mustard on one slice of bread and mayo on another.
- Drop a tbl of butter into your skillet and coat the bottom of your skillet once it melts. Drop your bread slices into the skillet (condiment side up) and fry until the side down begins to brown.
- Turn off the heat. Add sliced tomato to the mayo side, top with a cheese slice, fried bologna and the mustard side of the other piece of bread. Allow to sit in the skillet (turning once) until the cheese melts.
- Slice and serve. Sigh....

OTHER EASY SANDWICHES

Easy mid-day meals were a staple in our household when I was growing up. The day was full so you better be able to put something together for yourself (and your siblings) if you got hungry before momma was ready to put a meal together. Here are a few of our favorite "easy to throw together" sandwiches. They all use white bread... why even try to make anything healthier at this point... and, to be fair, they are tastier this way. Why spoil a good thing?

❖ Tomato Sandwich

To make this sandwich truly amazing, you will need warm, sun ripened tomatoes straight from the garden, Miracle Whip, and a really good / soft sliced white bread. Slice that tomato into medium thick slices, put Miracle Whip on both bread slices, layer on the tomato, dust with salt and pepper and dig in! My mouth is watering just thinking about it.

❖ Peanut Butter and Banana Sandwich

This is one of my man's favorites. Go again with the sliced white bread adding peanut butter, sliced bananas and, if you just want to go crazy, a little jelly. Smash that thing together and eat it as is or give it a light grill if you want to warm it up. Yum!

❖ Cucumber Sandwich

I am using my favorite herbs but you can throw whatever you might prefer in here. For my favorite version, mix together a packet of softened cream cheese with 1 tbl each of tarragon, parsley and chives. Add a little salt and pepper to taste. Clean and thinly slice a fresh cucumber. Assemble the sandwich on white bread by spreading each half of the bread with the cream cheese mixture, layering on the cucumber slices, pressing the sides together and removing the crusts. These are easiest to eat if you cut them into 3 finger sized pieces or you quarter your sandwich. My mouth is watering! Definitely making these this week!

Salads & Sides

COLESLAW

(MAYONNAISE AND VINEGAR STYLES)

Coleslaw starts the same type of arguments as deviled eggs in our house. Some prefer the vinegar style and others the mayonnaise (or Miracle Whip) version. Whichever you prefer, you should give the other a chance to impress every once in a while. Did you know that your taste buds are replaced every 2 weeks (roughly) and that over time some are not replaced? This changes the way you "taste" things and creates opportunities for you to try again things that you previously said "no way" to. Be adventurous!

❖ Ingredients (Mayo Option):

- White Cabbage - 1/2 head shredded
- Onion - 1/4 c chopped
- Sour Cream (or Plain Yogurt) - 1/2 c
- Mayonnaise (or Miracle Whip) - 1/2 c
- Dry Mustard - 1/2 tsp
- Seasoned Salt - 1/2 tsp
- Pepper - 1/8 tsp
- Sugar - 1 tsp

❖ Ingredients (Vinegar Option):

- White Cabbage - 1/2 head shredded
- Red Cabbage - 1/4 head shredded
- Red Onion - 1/2 small thinly sliced
- Carrot - 1 large peeled and shredded
- Canola Oil - 1/3 c
- Apple Cider Vinegar - 1/4 c
- Celery Seed - 1 tsp
- Salt - 1 tsp
- Pepper - 1/2 tsp
- Sugar - 1 tbl

❖ Tools:

- Medium Bowl with Lid
- Sharp Knife
- Measuring Cups and Spoons
- Cutting Board
- Small Mixing Bowl

❖ Directions:

- In a small bowl, mix together all of the wet and dry ingredients (not the vegetables).
- In a medium bowl, toss together all the vegetables.
- Add the contents of your small bowl (dressing) to the medium bowl with your veggies and mix thoroughly.
- Cover and refrigerate at least 1 hour.

CORN AND TOMATO SALAD

This is a super fresh and crunchy salad that is a great addition to any summertime meal. Pulling that corn fresh and making the salad immediately will give you a real "garden to table" flavor.

❖ Ingredients:

- Fresh Corn - 6 Ears
- Grape Tomatoes - 2 Cups
- Red Onion - 1/2
- Cilantro - 2 tbs
- Chives - 2 tbs
- Basil - 2 tbs
- White Wine Vinegar - 1/4 c
- Salt and Pepper

❖ Tools:

- Sharp Knife
- Chopping Board
- Large Bowl with Lid
- Roasting Pan (Optional)

❖ Directions:

- Shuck and CLEAN your corn removing any remaining silk
- Optional - Lightly roast your ears of corn on the grill or in the oven.
- Cut the corn from the cobs and put in a large bowl.
- CLEAN and halve your tomatoes and toss halves with corn.
- Rough chop your herbs and add to the bowl. Toss the salad.
- Add your white wine vinegar.
- Add salt and pepper to taste and toss salad until blended thoroughly.
- Refrigerate for at least 1 hour before serving.

DEVILED EGGS

Our family fights over deviled eggs. We fight over how many each person gets and also whether they are made with mayo or Miracle Whip. The solution to all this is that we make both versions and we make A LOT of them so that people are not throwing elbows to grab their eggs!

❖ Option 1 Ingredients:

- Eggs - 6 lrg
- Mayonnaise - 4 tbl
- Dry Mustard - 1/2 tsp
- Salt and Pepper - to taste
- Paprika

❖ Option 2 Ingredients:

- Eggs - 6 lrg
- Miracle Whip - 4 tbl
- Sweet Pickle Relish - 1 tbl
- Salt and Pepper - to taste
- Paprika

❖ Tools:

- Medium Sauce Pan
- Small Bowl
- Hand Mixer
- Serving Plate
- Measuring Spoons

❖ Directions:

- Place eggs in the saucepan and add enough water to cover the eggs. Bring the water to a boil and allow to boil for 7 minutes.
- Remove the pan from the heat, run cold water over the eggs until it replaces the hot water. Add enough ice to cover the eggs and allow to sit for 3 minutes.
- Shell, halve and separate the eggs placing the yolks in the small bowl and the white halves on the serving plate.
- Using a fork, mash the egg yolks.
- Add all other ingredients and mix with a blender until smooth.
- Using a spoon, fill your egg white halves with the mixture and finish with a sprinkle of paprika.

COUSIN LYNLEE'S 9 LAYERED SALAD

LET'S TALK ABOUT COUSIN LYNLEE! SHE WON'T MIND! This is one BEAUTIFUL woman! Doesn't it seem like my family is full of these?? ;) She is married to my husband's cousin, the distiller (Leiper's Fork Distillery), she is raising two rambunctious boys and helping to run the distillery. How she has time to mind her chickens, ride her horses, tend to everything else and manage to cook too is just beyond me, but she clearly can! This is a busy mom's dish. It is really yummy day one but is just one of those dishes that is even better day two. Try it y'all!

❖ Ingredients:

- Lettuce - 1/2 head shredded or 1 bag
- Celery - 3 stalks
- Red Onion - 1/4 lrg
- Baby Peas - 1 can
- Mayonnaise - 1 1/2 c
- Eggs - 4 lrg
- Bacon - 6 slices
- Parmesan Cheese
- Salt and Pepper

❖ Tools:

- Sharp Knife
- Cutting Board
- Large Round Serving Dish

❖ Directions:

- Chop celery and red onion finely.
- Boil eggs 8 minutes, peel, cool and chop.
- Cook bacon until crispy. Let cool and then crumble.
- Layer ingredients in serving dish in the order listed.
- Sprinkle with grated Parmesan cheese.
- Add a dash of salt and pepper.
- Chill before serving, and then DIG IN!

MOMMA DOT'S LIME JELLO SALAD

Momma Dot was a quintessential Southern Woman of her time. She would be fully dolled up just to cook a meal. I never saw her looking less than perfect. In her later years, she had this beautiful white hair (that both of her children inherited) that was always perfection and she had a natural grace that was both in spirit and body. This cookbook would not be complete without her being represented and so we present the "Lime Jell-O Salad" that she would prepare while looking like June Cleaver. Love you Momma Dot!

❖ Ingredients:

- Lime Jell-O - 1 small box
- Cream Cheese - 8 oz softened
- Boiling Water - 1/2 c
- Lemon Juice - 1 tsp
- Mayonnaise - 1 tsp
- Crushed Pineapple - small can with juice
- Evaporated Milk - 1/2 c
- Chopped Pecans - 1 c

❖ Tools:

- Glass Bowl or Baking Dish
- Hand Mixer or Whisk
- Measuring Cups and Spoons

❖ Directions:

- Mix Jell-O and boiling water in glass bowl or dish.
- Add softened cream cheese and blend evenly.
- Add remaining ingredients one at a time, mixing each in thoroughly.
- Refrigerate until set.

MACARONI SALAD

Macaroni salad all day, every day. There are so many variations on this dish and I love them all. I literally cannot imagine a 4th of July picnic without macaroni salad. Now, my family will fight over whether it is prepared with mayonnaise or Miracle Whip... I will let YOU make that call for your brood.

❖ Ingredients:

- Macaroni - 2 c dried elbow or spiral
- Celery - 2 stalks
- Mayonnaise - 3/4 c
- Red Onion - 1 small
- Fresh Parsley or Dill - 1 tbl chopped
- Dried Mustard - 1/2 tsp
- Sugar - 1 tsp
- Cider Vinegar - 1 tbl
- Salt and Pepper - to taste

❖ Tools:

- Large Pot
- Large Mixing Bowl
- Sharp Knife
- Cutting Board
- Measuring Cups and Spoons

❖ Directions:

- Cook, drain, rinse and cool pasta according to directions.
- Dice celery and onion (you only need 1/4 c of onion) and chop your herb of choice.
- In your large bowl, mix together the mayo, dried mustard, sugar, cider vinegar, salt and pepper.
- Add the pasta and chopped vegetables to the bowl and blend gently but thoroughly.
- Cover and refrigerate for up to 3 days (but I bet it doesn't last that long!)

AUNT NANCY'S CHUTNEY DIP

Southerners are social people. We love to gather and food is always involved. Having a dish to contribute to these gatherings that is a little different, one that has not made appearances at every gathering since high school, becomes a competition of sorts. This one is a winner. It covers all the taste/texture profile requirements to make a girl happy: creamy and crunchy as well as salty and sweet. Trust me, this is WAY better than dumping your Junior Mints or Raisinets into your popcorn!

❖ Ingredients:

- Cream Cheese - 8 oz softened
- Mayonnaise - 1 c
- Green Onions - 2 diced
- Shredded Cheddar Cheese - 1 c
- Bacon - 4 slices
- Mango Chutney - 1 small jar

❖ Tools:

- Skillet (for bacon, or however you like to cook yours!)
- Mixing Bowl
- Glass Baking Dish

❖ Directions:

- Preheat oven to 350 degrees.
- Cook bacon, cool and crumble. Set aside.
- Mix cream cheese, mayonnaise, diced onions and cheddar cheese and spread evenly in bottom of baking dish.
- Spread chutney on top of mixture.
- Top with crumbled bacon.
- Bake for 20 minutes and let cool.
- Serve with Fritos Scoops!

Desserts

BAKING TIPS

- Sift your flour for the best results.
- Check expiration dates on your baking supplies (no one likes biscuits that turn out like "hard tack").
- When baking cakes, grease and flour the bottom and sides of the baking pans.
- Eggs should be at least 3 days old before using them in cake recipes.
- To make creamy icing, combine milk or cream and sugar, add one tsp of maple syrup for each cup of sugar and boil as usual.

PIE CRUST

Why buy a pie crust when you can make your own easily (and know for sure what is in it). Pie crusts are amazingly simple to make and are very versatile. A pie crust can be the basis for a breakfast dish like quiche, a dinner dish like Chicken Pot Pie or a dessert like pies (or small fried pies...yummy).

❖ Ingredients: (for a standard 8-9" crust)

- Flour - 1 c (plus a little for rolling it out)
- Salt - 1/2 tsp
- COLD butter - 6 tbl
- ICE COLD water (I usually fill a cup half full with ice and add water)
- For a pastry to use with a dessert, add 1 teaspoon of sugar.

❖ Tools:

- Pastry Cutter (or two knives)
- Butter Knife
- Fork
- Measuring Cups and Spoons
- Large Bowl
- Rolling Pin
- Plastic Wrap

❖ Directions:

- Mix flour and salt (and sugar if this is a dessert pastry) in a large bowl.
- Cut COLD butter into small pieces and add to the dry mix. Use pastry cutter to cut the butter into the dry mix until they are the size of small peas.
- Slowly add cold water a tablespoon at a time, stirring with a fork each time until all of the flour has pulled together.
- With your hands, gather the dough and shape into a disk. Wrap in plastic wrap and refrigerate until you are ready to use.
- When ready, put the dough on a lightly floured surface and roll out to desired thickness. You may then cut to your purpose.

APPLE PIE

❖ Ingredients:

- Pastry for two 9" pie crusts (see page 96)
- Granny Smith Apples - 6 medium
- Sugar - 3/4 c
- Flour 1/4 c
- Cinnamon - 1/2 tsp
- Nutmeg - 1/2 tsp
- Allspice - 1/4 tsp
- Butter - 6 tbl
- Salt - 1/4 tsp

❖ Tools:

- Pie Plate
- Peeler
- Sharp Knife
- Measuring Cups and Spoons
- Cutting Board
- Large Mixing Bowl

❖ Directions:

- Preheat oven to 425 degrees.
- Prepare pastry.
- In a large mixing bowl, combine sugar, flour, salt, cinnamon, nutmeg and allspice.
- Wash, peel and thinly slice apples.
- Add apples to dry mixture and mix until all apples are coated.
- Roll out pastry dough and put bottom crust in the pie plate.
- Add apple mixture to the pie plate and dot with butter.
- Cover with top pie crust and seal edges. If you are not doing a lattice as shown, make sure you cut venting slits in the top.
- Bake 40-50 minutes or until the crust is brown and the juices are bubbling.

APPLE FRIED PIES

❖ Ingredients:

- "Dessert" Pie Crust (COLD)
- All-Purpose Flour - 1/4-1/2 c
- Honeycrisp Apples - 2 medium
- Sugar - 1 tbl
- Salt - 1/4 tsp
- Nutmeg - 1/2 tsp
- Cinnamon - 1/2 tsp
- Allspice - 1/2 tsp
- Unsalted Butter - 2 tbl
- Canola Oil - 1/4 c

❖ Tools:

- Measuring Spoons
- Spatula
- Cast Iron Skillet
- Small Sauté Pan
- Small Bowl
- Rolling Pin
- Pizza Cutter
  (or a bowl with a neat edge)

❖ Directions:

- Peel, slice and rough chop apples.
- Put chopped apples in a bowl and add sugar, salt, nutmeg, cinnamon and allspice. Mix well.
- Melt butter in a small sauté pan over medium heat. Add the apple mixture and cook until the apples begin to soften. Set aside and allow to cool.
- Turn the pie dough out onto a dry, clean and floured surface. Roll out "dessert" pie crust to 1/8" deep and cut into 8" circles with either a pizza cutter or a bowl with a neat edge.
- Fill the pastry circles with 2-3 tablespoons of the apple mixture, fold the pie dough over the apples to make half moons and seal edges with the back of a fork.
- Heat approximately 1/4" canola oil in a cast iron skillet over medium heat. When the oil begins to shimmer a little, add your apples filled pastry. Cook until brown (2-3 minutes), turn and brown the other side. Remove to paper towels to drain and serve immediately.
- Serving Tip: These are especially nice with a little powdered sugar or cinnamon sugar sprinkled on top or with a little dollop of vanilla ice cream.

Variations: You can substitute peaches, apricots, and other sturdy fruits for the apples to create other fried pie options (make sure to adjust or eliminate spices as needed). You can also use chopped chocolate or caramel to make especially decadent fried pies!

BANANA BREAD

Did you know that there is a National Banana Bread Day? There is! It is February 23rd. On this day, MILLIONS of Americans are baking, consuming and appreciating the creativity involved in the development of this 1930s recipe. Well....maybe not millions. After all, you need ripe bananas for this recipe and you would be pretty amazing if you could time that out just right to observe the date. I may try that next year. That is wh-a-t I n-e-e-d. Another day to justify eating things that should be reserved as "once in a while" to preserve what little figure I have left!

Undoubtedly, this is one of the most popular things that I bake. I have shared this recipe many, many times over the last 30 years. Serve it up and see if you are not asked to share the recipe too!

❖ Ingredients:

1 2/3 c Flour, 1 tsp Baking Soda, 1/4 tsp Baking Powder, 1/2 tsp Salt, 1 c Sugar, 1/3 c Butter (softened) plus extra to grease the Loaf Pan, 2 Eggs, 4 medium ripe mashed Bananas, 1/3 c Water, 1/2 chopped Nuts (optional)

❖ Tools:

Electric Mixer, Loaf Pan, Mixing Bowl, Spatula, Measuring Cups and Spoons

❖ Directions:

Heat oven to 350 degrees. Grease the bottom of the loaf pan (I prefer a ceramic or glass loaf pan). In a small bowl, blend together dry ingredients except sugar and nuts. Mix sugar and 1/3 c softened butter in your mixing bowl until thoroughly blended. Add the eggs to this mixture and mix again until thoroughly blended. Add mashed bananas and water and beat for 30 seconds. Stir in the mixed dry ingredients (except nuts) and mix until just blended. If you like nuts, stir them in now (I prefer pecans). Pour into the loaf pan and bake for 50 to 60 minutes or until a toothpick inserted into the center comes out clean. Remove from the oven, allow to cool for 5-10 minutes, loosen sides with a butter knife and allow to cool completely before slicing.

BANANA PUDDING

Some things can be done with shortcuts and be just fine but Banana Pudding IS NOT ONE OF THEM. Truly delicious Banana Pudding must be prepared with homemade custard (and real deal Nilla Wafers). No other way produces the richness and creaminess that you really need for this dessert to succeed spectacularly. Do yourself a favor and ditch the boxed pudding mix on this one.

- Ingredients - 1 Box Nilla Vanilla Wafers, 4-6 good sized Bananas (no green on the "nanner" please), 7 Eggs (separated), 4 c Milk, 1 tsp Vanilla, 2/3 c Flour, 1/8 tsp Salt, 1 c + 1/2 c Sugar, 3/4 tsp Cream of Tartar (optional)

- Tools - Double Boiler, Whisk, Measuring Cups and Spoons, Large Oven Safe Bowl, Knife, 1 large and one small Glass Bowl, Spatula and Hand Mixer

- Directions for Custard - Fill bottom pan of Double Boiler with water until it reaches the fill line (or touches about the bottom 1" of the top pan). Separate your eggs putting the egg yolks in the smaller bowl and the egg whites in the larger bowl. Begin to heat the water in your double boiler pan to boiling. Add Sugar, Flour and Salt to the top pan of your double boiler and blend this dry mixture with your whisk. In your smaller bowl, gently mix your egg yolks until they are blended and then blend in your milk. Slowly, while constantly whisking, add your liquid mixture to your dry mixture. This is the hard part, you must keep slowly whisking until the mixture begins to thicken. This can take 10-20 minutes depending upon humidity (I once tried to make this in the Bahamas...tasty but not exactly perfect). Note: if your pan begins to spit hot water at you, turn the heat down A LITTLE. If you turn it down too much, your custard will not cook. Once the custard begins to stick thickly to your whisk, it is time to remove it from the heat and add your vanilla extract. Blend thoroughly and set aside.

- Directions for Meringue - Break out your hand mixer and start mixing your egg whites and cream of tartar on high speed until foamy. Begin adding the sugar slowly. Continue to mix on high speed until stiff peaks are formed. Set aside.

- Composition and Completion - Preheat Oven to 350 degrees. Add a little custard to the bottom of your large oven safe bowl and then begin layering: wafers, banana slices, custard, wafers, banana slices, custard ... you get the idea ... until you run out of custard (this should be the last layer). Cover the whole shebang with your meringue. Make sure that meringue goes from edge to edge sealing everything in and make cute little peaks with the back of a spoon to make it look really special. Pop that thing in the oven (top of the dish should be in the top third of the oven) and watch carefully. When the meringue peaks begin to brown, your banana pudding ready. I let mine sit about 20 minutes prior to serving.

- NOTE: Remember that we are using eggs in this dish. This means that you must refrigerate your left overs. This dish is not as delish day two but this may not be a problem. If your family is like mine, none will be left to refrigerate.

RHUBARB PIE

❖ Ingredients:

- Deep Dish Pie Crust – 2 (see page 96)
- Rhubarb – 6 cups cut
- Sugar – 2 c
- Salt – 1/8 tsp
- Allspice – 1/4 tsp
- Flour – 2/3 c
- Butter – 3 tbl
- Grated Orange Peel – 1 tsp

❖ Tools:

- Deep Pie Plate
- Sharp Knife
- Cutting Board
- Large Mixing Bowl
- Measuring Cups and Spoons

❖ Directions:

- Preheat oven to 425 degrees.
- Clean, trim, and chop the rhubarb into 1/2 inch pieces.
- In a large mixing bowl, blend together the sugar, flour, allspice, salt and grated orange peel.
- Add the rhubarb to the dry mixture and blend to coat well.
- Transfer to a pastry lined pie plate, dollop with butter chunks, and cover with a second pie crust, sealing the edges tightly.
- Cut slits in the top pie crust to vent and bake 50-55 minutes or until the crust is nice and brown and the juices from the pie are bubbling through the top.

COBBLER

Cobblers are quick to throw together and very versatile. All types of fruit can be incorporated into a cobbler. This is your basic Peach Cobbler, but you should definitely experiment with cherries, blackberries, apples... AND if you really want to go "Southern," try a Strawberry-Rhubarb Cobbler. Oh my GOODNESS!

❖ Ingredients:

- Fresh Peaches - 6 peeled and sliced
- Sugar - 1/2 c + 1 1/2 tbl
- Cornstarch - 1 tbl
- Cinnamon - 1/4 tsp +1/4 tsp
- Lemon Juice - 1 tsp
- Butter - 3 tbl + 3 tbl
- Flour - 1 c
- Cornstarch - 1/4 tsp
- Baking Powder - 1 1/2 tsp
- Salt - 1/2 tsp
- Milk - 3/4 c - 1 c

❖ Tools:

- Measuring Spoons and Cup
- 2 Quart Casserole Dish
- Medium Sauce Pan
- Medium Bowl
- Pastry Cutter (or two knives)

❖ Directions:

- Heat oven to 400 degrees.
- Mix 1/2 c sugar, cornstarch and cinnamon in a saucepan.
- Stir in peaches and lemon juice and cook over medium-low heat until mixture thickens and boils. Boil for 1 minute and then remove from heat.
- Put 3 tbl butter in a 9x9 baking dish and place in oven.
- While the butter is melting in the oven, blend together the flour, 1 1/2 tbl sugar, baking powder, cornstarch, 1/4 tsp cinnamon, and salt and cut 3 tbl butter into the dry mixture until it looks like fine crumbs. Add the milk and blend thoroughly (it should be like a thick pancake batter).
- Pour the batter into the hot baking dish and pour the peaches over the batter.
- Sprinkle with cinnamon sugar and bake for 25 to 30 minutes or until bubbly and light brown.
- Tip: This is especially nice with a little dollop of vanilla ice cream.

COCONUT COOKIE BARS

❖ Ingredients:

- Butter - 8 tbl (or 1 stick)
- Graham Cracker Crumbs - 1 1/2 cups
- Chocolate Chips - 1 cup
- Flaked Coconut - 1 1/2 cup
- Sweetened Condensed Milk - 1 14 oz can
- Chopped Nuts - 1/2 to 1 cup
- Cooking Spray

❖ Tools:

- Measuring Cup
- Baking Dish
- Small Bowl
- Spatula

❖ Directions:

- Preheat oven to 350 degrees.
- Spray baking dish with no-stick cooking spray.
- Melt butter.
- Combine graham cracker crumbs with melted butter and press into bottom of your baking dish.
- Pour sweetened condensed milk evenly over the graham cracker crumb base.
- Layer on evenly the chocolate chips, coconut and finally the nuts.
- Bake for 20-30 minutes (until coconut lightly browns).
- Allow to cool and then cut into bars.
- DIG IN!

AUNT TILLIE'S COCONUT CAKE

This recipe takes no small amount of time. Given how much time it takes, imagine how special you would feel if the only time anyone had a chance to enjoy it was on YOUR BIRTHDAY! My brother was born on Christmas Eve and one of my Aunt Tillie's contributions to the Christmas Eve celebrations was to make this cake and designate it as Ricky's birthday cake. Only something that obviously requires this much patience and love could shift the focus from a holiday and make his day more special than it otherwise would seem to him. We are all scattered now and it has been a long time since I have enjoyed this cake. Maybe it is time to rustle one up and set aside some time to simply enjoy it and my memories. Make sure you are making time for your special memories. Sit, reflect, share and smile.

- Cake Ingredients - 2 sticks Butter (room temperature), 2 c Sugar, 4 lrg Eggs, 3 c sifted Flour, 2 1/2 tsp Baking Powder, 1/2 tsp Salt, 1 c Milk, 1 tsp Almond Extract, 1 tsp Vanilla Extract
- Frosting Ingredients - 1 1/2 c Sugar, 1/2 tsp Cream of Tartar, 1/8 tsp Salt, 1/2 c HOT Water, 4 lrg Eggs (whites only at room temperature), 1/2 tsp Almond Extract, 1/2 tsp Coconut Extract (optional), 1 c Coconut Flakes
- Tools - Electric Mixer, Spatulas, Measuring Cups and Spoons, Multiple Mixing Bowls, three 9" Round Cake pans, Heavy Saucepan, Candy Thermometer, Special Cake Plate
- Cake Instructions - Preheat oven to 375 degrees. Grease and flour the cake pans. Combine flour, baking powder and salt in a bowl and set aside. Measure out the milk and set aside. In a separate bowl, cream the butter; gradually add the sugar beating well at medium speed between additions. Add the eggs one at a time beating well after each addition. Alternating the dry mixture and the milk, begin to add these ingredients to the creamed mixture. Mix in the almond and vanilla extracts. Pour the batter into your prepared cake pans and bake for 20 to 25 minutes or until a toothpick inserted into the middle of the cake comes out clean. Remove from the oven and allow to cool for 10 minutes. Remove the cake from the pans by inverting them over wire racks and allow to cool completely.
- Frosting Instructions - Combine your sugar, cream of tartar, and salt in a heavy saucepan. Mix in the water and cook over medium heat while stirring constantly until it is clear. Continue to cook WITHOUT stirring until it reaches 240 degrees. Remove from heat. Separate eggs and beat the egg whites until fluffy. While continuing to beat the eggs, slowly start incorporating the syrup mixture. Add the almond extract and continue beating until the frosting is thick enough to spread.
- Composition - Arrange your first layer cake on the cake plate. Add a thin layer of icing and a light dusting of coconut. Top with your second layer and repeat icing and coconut sprinkle. Finish with the third layer and frost the entire cake sprinkling with the remaining coconut to complete.
- Voilà! Love in a cake.

FUDGE PIE TWO WAYS

Ever heard of a Pie Contest? Not pie eating... pie making. This is serious business here in the South and a staple of the summer fairs from my childhood. The competition was fierce and grudges could be developed that would go on for generations. Well, maybe I am exaggerating a LITTLE. It was never something so serious that it could not be solved over a cup of coffee and a slice of pie. The two recipes shown below belong to my grandmother, GG, and my Aunt Biba. A bake-off between these two was only to our benefit!

Grandma Brown's Version

❖ Ingredients:

- 1 Deep Dish Pie Crust (see page 96), 4 lrg Eggs, 2 tbl White Karo Syrup, 1 1/2 c Sugar, 1/4 tsp Salt, 1 tsp Vanilla Extract, 1 stick (1/2 c) Butter, 3 squares Unsweetened Chocolate

❖ Tools:

- Deep Pie Plate, Medium Mixing Bowl, Small Saucepan, Measuring Cups and Spoons, Electric Mixer

❖ Directions:

- Preheat oven to 325 degrees. Beat together the eggs, syrup, sugar, salt and vanilla. In a small saucepan, melt together the chocolate squares and butter over low heat. Blend the chocolate / butter mixture into the sugar mixture and pour into a pastry lined pie plate. Bake for 40-45 minutes.

Aunt Biba's Version

❖ Ingredients:

- 1 Deep Dish Pie Crust (see page 96), 2 lrg Eggs, 1 c Sugar, 1/4 c Flour, 1/4 c Cocoa, 1 tsp Vanilla Extract, 1 stick (1/2 c) Butter

❖ Tools:

- Deep Pie Plate, Medium Mixing Bowl, Small Mixing Bowl, Small Saucepan, Measuring Cups and Spoons, Electric Mixer

❖ Directions:

- Preheat oven to 350 degrees. Mix together all dry ingredients. Beat eggs in a small bowl. Melt butter. Blend together the dry ingredients, beaten eggs, vanilla extract and melted butter. Pour into a pastry lined pie plate. Bake for 30-40 minutes.

NANA'S PEANUT BUTTER BALLS

Christmas is just not the same without Nana's peanut butter balls. She has made them every Christmas for as long as I remember, and they are always delicious. They are definitely a favorite of my husband's! However, as the years (decades) have gone by and the family has grown, we have definitely come to understand that they are a "first come first served" type of dessert. If you don't hurry, you are just out of luck!

❖ Ingredients:

- Peanut Butter - 1 c
- Butter - 8 tbl (or 1 stick)
- Graham Cracker Crumbs - 2/3 c
- Powdered Sugar - 2 c
- Chocolate Chips - 9 oz

❖ Tools:

- Measuring Cup and Spoons
- Cookie Sheet
- Medium Mixing Bowl
- Spatula
- Electric Mixer
- Small Microwave Safe Bowl
- Parchment Paper

❖ Directions:

- Put your peanut butter and room temperature butter in a medium mixing bowl and combine on medium speed with your hand mixer until smooth.
- Add 1/3 of the graham cracker crumbs and 1/4 of the powdered sugar and blend on low speed until evenly incorporated. Continue to add graham cracker crumbs and powdered sugar until fully incorporated and smooth (it will be THICK).
- Using a tablespoon, scoop out the mixture and roll into balls with your (clean) hands. You should have between 25-30 balls.
- Place them on a parchment paper lined cookie sheet and place in the refrigerator for at least 30 minutes.
- In a small microwave safe bowl, melt your chocolate chips, stopping to stir frequently. Note: you may need to add some butter to keep this fluid and smooth.
- Dip each of your cold peanut butter balls in the melted chocolate and return to the parchment paper to cool.
- Store in the refrigerator for up to a week. DELISH!

PECAN PIE

This was, for many years, one of my contributions to our Thanksgiving celebrations. For a young mom, it was super easy to make and could be made a tad bit more special by arranging the pecans "just so" on the top to create a special presentation. There are as many ways to modify/enhance this pie as your imagination can come up with. One of my husband's favorite variations adds chocolate chips to the mix. What sounds good to you?

❖ Ingredients:

- Deep Dish Pie Crust – 1 (store bought or see page 96)
- Pecans – 1 1/2 c whole or chopped
- Light Corn Syrup – 1 c
- Eggs – 3 lrg
- Butter – 3 tbl
- Sugar – 1 c
- Vanilla Extract – 1 tsp

❖ Tools:

- Deep Pie Plate
- Medium Mixing Bowl
- Whisk
- Measuring Cups and Spoons
- Electric Mixer

❖ Directions:

- Preheat oven to 350 degrees.
- Melt butter.
- In a small mixing bowl, whisk together your eggs.
- In a medium mixing bowl, mix together the corn syrup, sugar, vanilla extract and melted butter.
- Incorporate your whisked eggs into the sugar mixture.
- Now for the pecans. If using chopped pecans, you can stir them directly into the liquid mixture, transfer it all to the pastry lined pie plate and bake. If using whole pecans, I suggest pouring MOST of the liquid mixture into the pastry lined pie plate reserving a little. Arrange the whole pecans nicely over the top of the pie and then pour the remaining liquid over the whole shebang.
- This should bake for 50- 65 minutes or until the center puffs up nicely.

AUNT ANN'S FRUIT CAKE

Christmas with my Mom's family would not have been the same without my Aunt Ann's Fruit Cake. I know that these tend to have a bad reputation but I loved hers. Time for another story!

On Christmas Eve, we would all gather at my grandmother's home on Park Avenue in Nashville. Grandma would make sure that all of her grandchildren's favorite dishes were represented on the kitchen table and counters (small kitchen and a large brood). While Grandma, Mom and the Aunts were organizing the food, we would sit outside and wait on Santa Claus (my Great Uncle George Hunter – Aunt Mackie's man) to arrive. There was a radio tower near to Park Avenue that had a red light on the top and we would swear that it was Rudolf and that the light was coming closer to us. It never occurred to us that the light was still there long after "Santa" had come and gone. Childhood is sometimes blissfully simple.

Aunt Ann's Fruit Cake was always there on Christmas Eve. It's a tradition that passed with my Grandmother and one that I sorely miss.

❖ Ingredients:

- Pecans – 1 lb
- Candied Cherries – 1 lb
- Pineapple – 1 lb
- Golden Raisins – 1 lb
- Orange – 1
- Lemon - 1
- Flour – 1 1/2 c
- Sugar – 1 c
- Baking Powder – 1/2 tsp
- Salt – 1/4 tsp
- Butter – 1/2 lb + 2 tbl
- Eggs – 5 lrg
- Vanilla Extract – 1 1/2 tbl
- Lemon Flavoring – 1 1/2 tbl

❖ Tools:

- Mixer
- Large, Medium and Small Mixing Bowls
- Bundt or Loaf Pan
- Spatula
- Sharp Knife
- Parchment Paper

❖ Directions:

- Preheat oven to 300 degrees.
- Halve the cherries and chunk the pineapple into bite size pieces. Zest the orange and lemon. Place the zest, whole nuts and all of the fruit in a medium mixing bowl , top with 1/2 cup of flour and toss until blended well.
- Mix 1 cup of flour, baking powder and salt in a small bowl and set aside.
- In a large mixing bowl, cream together the sugar and butter. Blend in the eggs one at a time. Add and blend in the lemon and vanilla flavoring.
- Slowly, mix in the dry mixture. When blended thoroughly, add the fruit mixture and again blend thoroughly.
- Using 2 tablespoons of butter, thoroughly butter your parchment paper and line your pan.
- Transfer the Fruit Cake mixture to the pan, place the filled pan in a water bath (another pan with about 1" of water in it) and place in the oven to cook at 300 degrees for approximately half an hour. Reduce the temperature to 250 degrees and cook for a further 2 1/2 hours.
- Remove, cool, slice and serve! Welcome to a slice of my childhood Christmas!

SWEET POTATO PIE

❖ Ingredients:

- Deep Dish Pie Crust – 1 (see page 96)
- Sweet Potatoes – 2 lrg
- Eggs – 4 lrg
- Butter – 1/4 c (1/2 stick)
- Sugar – 1 1/2 c
- Milk – 1/2 c
- Vanilla Extract – 2 tsp
- Cinnamon – 1 tsp
- Nutmeg – 1/2 tsp

❖ Tools:

- Deep Pie Plate
- Medium Mixing Bowl
- Small Mixing Bowl
- Medium Saucepan
- Measuring Cups and Spoons
- Electric Mixer

❖ Directions:

- Preheat oven to 350 degrees.
- Place the sweet potatoes in a medium saucepan whole and add enough water to cover them.
- Bring it to a boil and cook the sweet potatoes until fork tender.
- Remove sweet potatoes from the water to cool then peel, cut into chunks and mash together with the butter, sugar, nutmeg, cinnamon and vanilla extract. Get a good mash on this!
- Beat together the eggs and milk in a separate bowl. Slowly, incorporate this into the sweet potato mixture.
- Beat briskly until creamy and smooth.
- Pour into a pastry lined pie plate and bake until firm (approximately 35-40 minutes).

SWEETENED WHIPPED CREAM

I know that I don't have to tell you that there are many uses for whipped cream. (Cut that out! I know what you're thinking!) Whipped Cream can be used to finish a dessert, top a hot chocolate or a hot (or cold) coffee "beverage," or to make a simple serving of jello special. This is not complicated, and it does not come from a can or container of dubious origins with dubious ingredients and of a dubious age. "Just Say Yes" to homemade Whipped Cream.

❖ Ingredients:

- Whipping Cream (chilled) - 1 c
- Sugar - 2 tbl
- Optional Flavoring (Almond Extract, Vanilla Extract, Grated Lemon, Ginger, etc) - 1/2 - 1 tsp

❖ Tools:

- Mixing Bowl
- Hand Mixer
- Spatula
- Measuring Spoons

❖ Directions:

- Add whipping cream to a medium chilled mixing bowl.
- Beat on high while slowly adding sugar (and optional flavoring) until firm peaks form.
- Cover and chill until ready to use.

STRAWBERRY SHORTCAKE

❖ Filling Ingredients:

- Ripe Strawberries - 1 quart sliced
- Sugar - 1 c

❖ Shortcake Ingredients:

- COLD Butter - 1/3 c
- Flour - 2 c + 1/2 c more for kneading
- Sugar - 2 1/2 tbl
- Baking Powder - 3 tsp
- Salt - 1 tsp
- Milk - 3/4 c

❖ Tools:

- Pastry Cutter
- Sharp Knife
- Mixing Bowl
- Cookie Sheet
- Parchment Paper

❖ Filling Directions:

- Combine sliced strawberries and sugar, cover and refrigerate.

❖ Shortcake Directions:

- Preheat oven to 425 degrees.
- Combine dry ingredients, cut the butter into the dry mix with the pastry cutter until the butter is a fine crumble.
- Add the milk and stir gently until just incorporated.
- Turn out onto a floured surface and fold and knead 15-20 times.
- Roll out to 1/2" thickness and cut with a biscuit cutter (or just about anything else you can imagine).
- Place on the parchment covered cookie sheet and bake for 8-10 minutes (until a light brown). Remove and cool.

❖ Serving Suggestion:

- Break the shortcake in half.
- Cover the bottom half with filling, cover this with sweetened whip cream (see previous page) and place the other half of the shortcake on top.
- Sprinkle with powdered sugar.

AUNT GLADYS' STRAWBERRY PIE

Oh my! It is not summertime without experiencing a beautiful strawberry pie. These are especially sweet when you take the time to actually go out and pick your own fresh, just ripened strawberries. This is a really fun excursion with small children, and there are many fun stories from my childhood that revolve around berry picking. The only problem with this plan is that you may not make it home with enough strawberries for your pie!

❖ Ingredients:

- Deep Dish Pie Crust – 1 (store bought or see page 96)
- Fresh Strawberries – 4 cups (whole)
- Sugar – 1 c
- Cornstarch – 3 tbl
- Strawberry Jell-O Mix – 3 tbl
- Boiling Water – 1 c
- Red Food Coloring – 2 drops

❖ Tools:

- Deep Pie Plate
- Sharp Knife
- Colander
- Whisk
- Small Saucepan
- Measuring Cups and Spoons

❖ Directions:

- Preheat oven to 350 degrees. Pre-bake and cool your pie crust. You should bake it until it is just turning brown (make sure the center is cooked through).
- Wash and trim your whole berries and leave in a colander to drain.
- In your saucepan, mix together the sugar, cornstarch, and strawberry Jell-O mix.
- Add the hot water and food coloring and bring to a boil stirring constantly for 1 minute.
- Add your berries to the pre-cooked pie crust and pour the filling mixture over the berries. Cover and refrigerate until cold before topping with some beautiful whipped cream and serving with a tall glass of iced tea!

Breads

CORNBREAD / CORN CAKES

Cornbread and Corn Cakes (or Hoe Cakes) are a staple in historical southern cooking. They are quick and easy to make and use inexpensive and easy to obtain ingredients. They are a favorite with barbecue, white beans (with chow-chow of course) and greens but are also yummy with most any other dinner you might prepare as a substitute for regular bread. For example, I LOVE me some Chili poured over a crunchy piece of Cornbread (cheater's Corn Pone Pie). Give it a try!

Cornbread

❖ Ingredients:

- 1 1/2 c Yellow Corn Meal, 1/2 c Flour, 1/4 c + 2 tbl melted Bacon Fat, 1 1/2 c Buttermilk, 1 tbl Baking Powder, 1/2 tsp Baking Soda, 1 tsp Sugar, 1 tsp Salt, 2 Eggs (Whipped)

❖ Tools:

- Large and Small Mixing Bowls, Cast Iron Skillet, Egg Whip, Measuring Cups and Spoons

❖ Directions:

- Preheat oven to 450 degrees.
- Add 2 tbl Bacon Grease to the cold skillet and put the skillet in the oven. While the skillet is heating up, mix your dry ingredients together in the mixing bowl.
- Whip your eggs and blend thoroughly your other wet ingredients. Add your wet ingredients to the dry ingredients and stir until just blended.
- Pour into a hot skillet (it should sizzle when you pour it in) and bake for 25-35 minutes.

Corn Cakes (aka Hoe Cakes)

❖ Ingredients:

- 1 1/2 Yellow Corn Meal, 1/2 c Flour, 2 tsp Baking Powder, 3/4 tsp Salt, 1 Egg (Whipped), 1/4-1/3 c Canola Oil, 1 1/4 c Water

❖ Tools:

- Large Mixing Bowl, Cast Iron Skillet (or Griddle), Egg Whip, Measuring Cups and Spoons

❖ Directions:

- Add some canola oil to the skillet and preheat skillet (or griddle) over medium to medium-high heat.
- While the skillet is heating up, mix your dry ingredients together in the mixing bowl. Whip your egg and water thoroughly together. Add your wet ingredients to the dry ingredients and stir until just blended.
- Ladle onto a hot skillet (it should sizzle when you pour it in) and cook for around 3 minutes on each side (the edges should be crispy). Serve immediately!

Variations: Add Jalapeño, Corn, or Cheese to your mixture.

WHITE LOAF BREAD

Occasionally (like when you are having 2nd Day Pot Roast Hash), store brought bread just will not do. In those cases, you will be much happier with your dinner if you take the time to make your own bread that you can cut into nice thick slices. This is your "I don't want thinly sliced bread" recipe!

❖ Ingredients:

- Flour - 6 - 7 c Sifted
- Sugar - 3 tbl
- Salt - 1 tbl
- Dry Yeast - 2 pkg (regular or quick-acting)
- Butter - 2 tbl (or 1/4 stick) softened
- Warm Water (120-130 degrees) - 2 1/4 c
- Cooking Spray

❖ Tools:

- Measuring Cup and Spoons
- Large Mixing Bowl
- Medium Mixing Bowl
- Loaf Pans (2)
- Hand Mixer

❖ Directions:

- Combine dry ingredients (3 1/2 c sifted flour, sugar, salt, yeast). Add softened butter and water (at 120-130 degrees). This temp is super important as it IS possible to kill your yeast. Kill the yeast and you kill the bread.
- Using your hand mixer, mix on low for 1 minute, scraping the sides frequently. Follow with mixing at medium speed for 1 minute.
- Stir in additional flour 1 c at a time until the dough is easy to handle.
- Turn the dough out onto a floured surface and knead (fold and press, fold and press...) for about 10 minutes.
- Grease a 2 1/2 quart bowl and put your dough in the bowl turning the greased side of the dough up. Cover with a kitchen towel and allow to rise in a warm place (I put mine in an oven that has been preheated to 125 and turned off) for 40-60 minutes or until doubled in size.
- Preheat oven to 425 degrees.
- Punch the dough down, divide into 2 halves and let rest for 5 minutes.
- Roll each half into 18x9" rectangles. Starting with the 9" wide end, fold down into thirds, turn with the open end at the top and roll tightly toward yourself and seal the end by pinching it closed.
- Place loaves seam side down in greased loaf pans. Brush the loaves lightly with melted butter and let rise 35-50 minutes or until doubled in size.
- Place on low rack (top of loaf should be mid oven) and bake for 25-30 minutes!

FAN YEAST ROLLS

These are a favorite with my German friends (particularly Gabriele) and my family. Of course, you can buy these frozen, thaw them out and bake them BUT it is not the same as making them yourself. THEY ARE JUST BETTER! Soooo, take a little extra time and pull these together yourself my friends. You will not regret it.

❖ Ingredients:

- Flour - 2 c Sifted + 1 1/2 to 1 13/4 more
- Sugar - 1/4 c
- Salt - 1 tsp
- Dry Yeast - 1 pkg (regular or quick-acting)
- Butter - 4 tbl (or 1/2 stick) softened + 2 tbl melted
- Egg - 1 slightly beaten
- Warm Water (120-130 degrees) - 1/2 c
- Warm Milk - 1/2 c scalded then cooled to 120 degrees
- Cooking Spray

❖ Tools:

- Measuring Cup and Spoons
- Baking Dish
- 2 Medium Mixing Bowls
- 2 Small Sauce Pans
- Hand Mixer

❖ Directions:

- Combine dry ingredients (2 c sifted flour, sugar, salt, yeast).
- Add 4 tbl softened butter, egg, water and milk (at 120 - 130 degrees). This temp is super important as it IS possible to kill your yeast. Kill the yeast and you kill the bread.
- Using your hand mixer, mix on low for 1 minute, scraping the sides frequently. Follow with mixing at medium speed for 1 minute.
- Stir in additional flour 1/4 c at a time until the dough is easy to handle.
- Turn the dough out onto a floured surface and knead (fold and press, fold and press...) for about 5 minutes.
- Grease a 2 1/2 quart bowl and put your dough in the bowl turning the greased side of the dough up. Cover with a kitchen towel and allow to rise in a warm place (I put mine in an oven that has been preheated to 125 and turned off) for 40-60 minutes or until doubled in size.
- Preheat oven to 400 degrees.
- Punch to dough down and roll out into a 1/2" deep rectangle. Brush entire surface with melted butter. Cut into 6 long strips about 1 1/2" wide, stack the strips on top of each other and cut the single consolidated strip into 1 - 1 1/2 pieces.
- Place the pieces cut side down in a greased muffin cup pan and bake for 10 to 16 minutes. Yum, yum!

A li'l Something Extra

AUNT ANN'S CHILI SAUCE

❖ Ingredients:

- Tomatoes - 12 lrg
- Green Bell Pepper - 2
- Onions - 2
- Sugar - 1 1/4 c
- Salt - 1 tbl
- Chili Powder - 2 tbl
- Cloves - 1 tsp
- Cinnamon - 2 1/2 tsp
- Vinegar - 1/2 c
- Hot Sauce - optional to taste

❖ Tools:

- Sharp Knife
- Cutting Board
- Large Pot with Lid
- Measuring Cups and Spoons

❖ Directions:

- Parboil tomatoes. If you've never done this, it's simple: clean the tomatoes, remove the stems, turn upside down and cut a shallow "X" on each tomato. Place the tomatoes in a bowl and pour boiling water over them. Remove to a shallow bath of cold water and then remove the skins.
- Chop bell peppers, onions and peeled tomatoes and place in a large pot.
- Add remaining ingredients to the pot, combine thoroughly, bring to a boil and then reduce heat to simmer. Cover and cook 3 hours.
- Use "as is" or blend in a blender for a finer sauce texture.

Here's what's cookin' Chili Sauce Serves
Recipe from the kitchen of Ann Hemmer
12 l peeled tomatoes
2 green peppers
2 onions
1 1/4 c sugar
1 Tbsp salt
1 tsp cloves
2 1/2 t. cinnamon
Cook 3 hrs
1/2 C vinegar

KATHY'S SUNDAY JAM (ALL WEEK)

❖ Ingredients:

- Fresh Strawberries – 5 1/2 c (prepared)
- Sugar – 5 c
- Pectin – 2 oz
- Butter – 1 tsp
- Lemon Juice – 2 tbl

❖ Tools:

- Sanitized Small Canning Jars (approx. 12) with NEW Lids and Rings
- Jar Rack for Water Bath
- Large Deep Pot with Lid
- Large Saucepan
- Ladle
- Funnel
- Canning Jar Lifter
- Potato Masher
- Magnetic Pen

❖ Directions:

- Prepare berries by washing, trimming and quartering.
- Measure out 5 cups of sugar and 5 1/2 cups of prepared berries using (VERY IMPORTANT) the same measuring cup. Do the sugar first.
- Place your jar rack into the large pot and add the canning jars and lids. Put enough water into the pot to allow the jars to sit in approximately 2" of water. Bring the water to a boil (180 degrees) and allow to boil while you are preparing the jam.
- While the jars are heating, add your strawberries and pectin to a large saucepan and heat over medium heat, stirring constantly, until it comes to a boil. Add the butter and lemon juice and bring back to a boil. Slowly add the sugar, constantly stirring, until it is all incorporated. Use a potato masher to break up any stubborn berries and bring to a third boil allowing to boil for 2 minutes. Remove from the heat.
- You are ready to can. Remove a hot jar from the pot using your jar lifter and a lid using the magnetic pen and place on a stable kitchen surface. Quickly, using the funnel and ladle, fill the jar to 1/4" from the top, seal tightly with a lid and ring and place back in the hot water. Do this until all the jars are filled. Once all the filled jars are back in the water, add enough water to slightly cover the tops and bring it back to a boil for 10 minutes.
- Remove the jars to a cooling rack and allow to reach room temperature before storing. The lids should not be "popped".

SUMMER GARDENS CREATE A LOT OF WORK, BUT OH MY, THE FRUITS OF THAT LABOR ARE WONDERFUL!

KATHY'S CANNED TOMATOES

These take some caution, time and talent but they are really a time saver when preparing future meals. These tomatoes can be used as salsa, a pasta sauce or the base for a really good vegetable soup. Kathy advises that it can look scary and that experience canning is helpful but you can never get the requisite experience if you don't start somewhere!

❖ Ingredients:

- Fresh Tomatoes – 12 lrg
- Onion – 3 lrg
- Green Bell Pepper – 2 lrg
- Red Bell Pepper – 1 med
- Yellow Bell Pepper – 1 med
- Garlic – 7 cloves
- Cumin – 2 1/2 tsp
- Coarse Pepper – 2 1/2 tsp
- Pickling Salt – 2 1/2 tbl
- Cilantro – 1/3 c
- Apple Cider Vinegar – 1 1/4 c
- Roasted Canned Tomato Sauce – 16 oz can
- Tomato Paste – 12 oz can

❖ Tools:

- Sanitized Large Canning Jars (approx. 8) with NEW Lids and Rings
- Wire Basket for Tomatoes
- 2 Large Deep Pots with Lid
- Large Saucepan
- Ladle
- Funnel
- Canning Jar Lifter
- Potato Masher
- Magnetic Pen

❖ Directions:

- Fill both large pots two-thirds full of hot water, put them on high heat and bring to a boil. Make sure your canning jars are free of nicks, cracks and sharp edges. Wash the jars, lids and wrings in hot, soapy water and rinse thoroughly.
- Place the clean jars, lids and rings in a pot of hot water and allow to simmer. Leave them there until needed. Wash tomatoes with cool water checking for any blemishes (no spots, cracks or growths).
- Fill the wire basket with tomatoes and lower it into the second pot of boiling water. Remove after 30 seconds and rinse with cold water. Repeat until all tomatoes have had their "hot bath".
- Prepare the tomatoes by cutting out the cores, removing the skins, trimming off any green spots and cutting into small chunks. Chop the onion and peppers. Mince the garlic.
- Place the prepared tomatoes, chopped vegetables, minced garlic, cumin, pepper, pickling salt, cilantro, apple cider vinegar, tomato sauce and tomato paste into a large saucepan and bring to a boil. Reduce the heat and allow to simmer for 20 minutes, stirring occasionally.
- Remove a clean jar, lid and ring from the hot water to a stable kitchen surface, fill the jar with the tomato mixture to within 1/2" of the top (head space), seal tightly and return to a pot of hot (not boiling) water. Repeat until you run out of tomato mixture. Fill the canning pot with enough water to just cover the tops of the canning jars, put the cover on the canning pot, bring the water to a boil and process for 40 minutes.
- Remove jars from the pot to a stable kitchen surface and allow to cool for about 12 hours before storing.

ONE OF THE WONDERFUL GIFTS OF SUMMER... CANNED TOMATOES

APPLESAUCE

Applesauce is NOT just for children. Don't believe me? Add a dollop of this applesauce along with a dab of sour cream to a crispy potato cake (see page 69) and then tell me that this is for babies!

❖ Ingredients:

- Granny Smith Apples - 4 lrg
- Cinnamon (or not) - 1/4 tsp
- Nutmeg (or not) - 1/8 tsp
- Sugar - 1/2 c
- Water - 1/2 c

❖ Tools:

- Peeler
- Sharp Knife
- Cutting Board
- Large Saucepan
- Measuring Spoons

❖ Directions:

- Clean, peel and core apples.
- Cut apples into large chunks.
- Place apples and water in saucepan and heat to boiling over medium heat.
- Reduce heat to simmer and cook, stirring to break up apples until they are fork tender.
- Stir in sugar, cinnamon and nutmeg and return to a boil. Boil until thickened.
- Remove from heat and cool.

ORANGE CRANBERRY SAUCE

I absolutely ADORE fresh cranberry sauce and I ABHOR the canned stuff. My philosophy: why suffer through something that I hate when I can make something really tasty in about 30 minutes? Just sayin'!

❖ Ingredients:

- Fresh Uncooked Cranberries - 2 8oz bags
- Oranges - 2 large Navel
- Sugar - 1/2 c
- Cinnamon - dash

❖ Tools:

- Medium Saucepan
- Zester
- Sharp Knife
- Medium Mixing Bowl

❖ Directions:

- Wash cranberries and discard any bad ones.
- Zest and juice oranges.
- Place cranberries, orange juice, orange zest, sugar and cinnamon in a medium saucepan over medium heat and simmer until the cranberries burst and the sauce thickens.
- Allow to cool before refrigerating.

BREAD & BUTTER PICKLES

Do you love sweet pickles? If so, you will adore these. Like all good things, they take some effort, but they are so much better than the store-bought that they are worth it!

❖ Ingredients:

- Cucumbers - enough for 6 quarts sliced
- Onions - enough for 1 quart sliced
- Sweet (Bell) Peppers - 4 lrg (mix colors)
- Salt - 1 c
- White Vinegar - 3 pints
- Sugar - 6 c
- Turmeric - 2 tbl
- Mustard Seed - 2 tbl
- Celery Seed - 2 tbl

❖ Tools:

- Canning Tools
- Jars, Lids and Rings
- Sharp Knife
- Cutting Board
- Large Pot

❖ Directions:

- Clean and slice cucumbers and sweet peppers into 1/4" slices. Peel and slice onions.
- Make a brine with 9 cups water and 1 cup salt, mix with vegetables and allow to stand for 3 hours.
- In a large pot, mix vinegar, sugar, turmeric, mustard seed and celery seed.
- Drain and add brined vegetables.
- Bring to a boil and remove from heat.
- Allow to cool and then put in jars.

Note: If you plan on these having a shelf life, please observe "canning protocols" when jarrin' these.

CONFETTI SALAD

This recipe is "OLD SCHOOL"! The elders in my family adore it but I have not seen it on a table in a while, so I was super excited to find this handwritten version. There is no attribution because frankly I cannot be sure of the author. However, I have a sneaking suspicion that this was from my Grandma Brown, lovingly referred to as "GG" by the next generation.

❖ Ingredients:

- Sauerkraut - 1 can
- Onion - 1 lrg
- Celery - 2 lrg stalks
- Pimentos - 1 can
- Green Bell Pepper - 1 med
- Sugar - 1 c

❖ Tools:

- Sharp Knife
- Cutting Board
- Large Bowl with Top

❖ Directions:

- Chop onion, celery, bell pepper and pimentos.
- Mix sauerkraut and chopped veg in a large bowl and top with sugar.
- Cover tightly and refrigerate overnight.

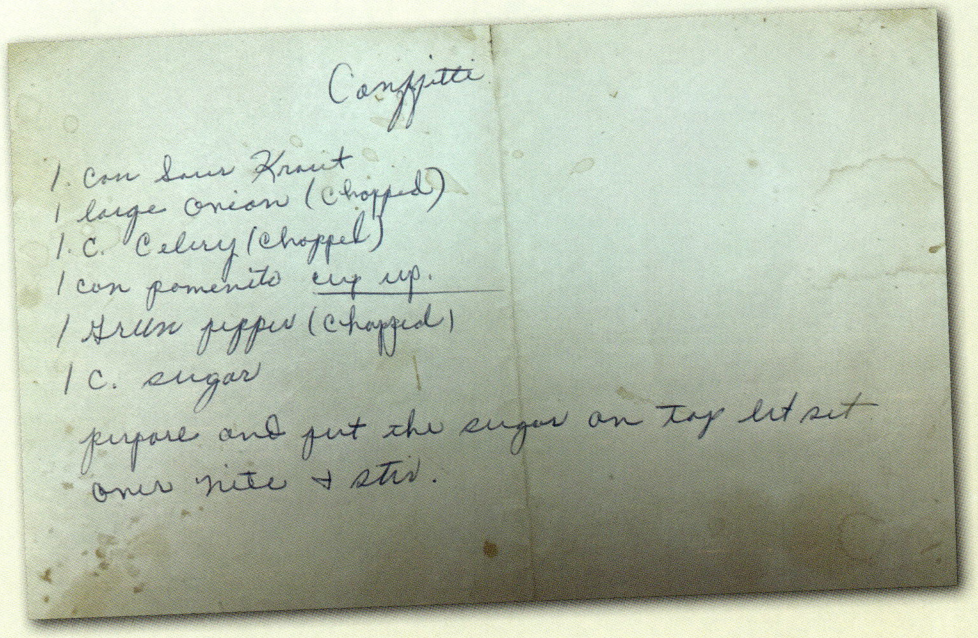

Conffetti

1. can Sour Kraut
1 large onion (chopped)
1. c. Celery (chopped)
1 can pomento cut up.
1 Green pepper (chopped)
1 c. sugar
prepare and put the sugar on top let set over nite & stir.

CHOW-CHOW

Chow-Chow is a cold relish most commonly made from a combination of chopped vegetables cooked down with spices and canned. The most common varieties are tomato or cabbage based and we Southerners use it adorn our pinto beans, hot dogs, hamburgers and just about anything else we think needs a little jazzing up. I would eat my grandmother's right out of the jar. Canning is involved with this recipe and, if you want it to have a good shelf life, you should follow Kathy's canning instructions for her tomatoes on page 124. Otherwise, put a lid on that thing, refrigerate it and eat it up quickly.

❖ Ingredients:

- White Distilled Vinegar – 5 c
- Sugar – 3 c
- Kosher Salt – 2 tbl
- Whole Cloves – 1 tbl
- Mustard Seed – 1 tbl
- Black Peppercorns – 1 tbl
- Mustard Powder – 1 tsp
- Turmeric – 1 tsp
- Bay Leaf - 1
- Green Tomatoes - 4 medium
- Green Bell Peppers - 2
- Red Bell Pepper - 1
- Vidalia Onion – 1 lrg
- Cabbage – 1/2 head

❖ Tools:

- Large Canning Jars, Lids and Rings
- Sharp Knife
- Cutting Board
- Large Saucepan/Pot

❖ Directions:

- Clean and sterilize all the canning jars, lids and rings.
- Put the vinegar, sugar, salt, cloves, mustard seed, peppercorns, mustard, turmeric and bay leaf into a large pot and simmer over medium heat, stirring occasionally, until the sugar dissolves and it becomes fragrant (5-10 minutes).
- While this is simmering, fine dice all of the vegetables and shred the cabbage.
- When the base is ready, add your cut vegetables to the mixture and bring to a boil. Reduce the heat to a simmer for 20 minutes. Remove from the heat, fish out the bay leaf and divide into your canning jars. Seal and refrigerate or begin eating right away!

CROUTONS

Store-bought croutons cannot beat homemade, so why waste your money? Day-old ciabatta or sourdough bread make DELICIOUS croutons, and it is so simple to do. DO IT! You will not regret it.

❖ Ingredients:

- Day-old Bread
- Olive Oil
- Optional Seasonings: I use garlic salt most frequently but have also been known to play with paprika, chili flakes, and herbs. Think about your accompanying dish and play with the flavors. PLAYING WITH YOUR FOOD IS FUN.

❖ Tools:

- Sharp Knife
- Cutting Board
- Spatula
- Large Mixing Bowl
- Baking Sheet

❖ Directions:

- Preheat oven to 375 degrees.
- Cut your bread into 1" cubes and place in your large mixing bowl.
- Pour Olive Oil over the bread cubes just enough to get a little on each piece of bread (you do not want to soak them in olive oil...they will be chewy instead of crispy) and then add your seasoning (if any).
- Mix it all up well (taste test here and adjust as needed) and then transfer to your baking sheet in a single layer.
- Bake for 7-12 minutes (or until they begin to brown).
- Taste test again (okay, this one is just for fun) to see if a little more browning is needed. When satisfied, remove from the oven and allow to cool in a single layer.

HOT BACON DRESSING

Over the years, I've found certain things to be absolutely true. One of these is that homemade salad dressing is better, hands down, than anything store bought. Sure, it takes some effort and the shelf life is not very long but the effort is worth it and you will not have to worry about shelf life because it will be gone in a trice. This is a Hot Bacon Dressing that can go over most any type of hardy green (iceberg, spinach, romaine, etc) and it also goes nicely over tart, fresh tomatoes too. If this seems a little too much trouble for you, mix together a good olive oil with 1/4 cup of fresh lemon juice, salt and pepper and a dollop of honey. Quick, fresh and easy.

❖ Ingredients:

- Bacon – 8 slices
- Red Wine Vinegar – 3 tbl
- Sugar – 1 tsp
- Dijon Mustard – 1/2 tsp
- Salt and Pepper – to taste

❖ Tools:

- Skillet
- Sharp Knife
- Cutting Board
- Whisk

❖ Directions:

- Cut your bacon into small pieces.
- Fry the bacon pieces over medium-low heat until crispy. Remove to paper towels to drain.
- With the skillet still over low heat, whisk in the red wine vinegar, sugar and Dijon mustard. Salt and pepper to taste.
- Remove from the heat and allow to cool slightly.
- Add back in your bacon bits and pour over your prepared salad.
- Serve immediately.

SPICED TEA

This hot tea recipe has been used in my family for at least 5 decades. We drink it when we have the flu, when it is cold and rainy, or when we want something in which to hide the whiskey. It is yummy 100% of the time.

❖ Ingredients:

- Instant Tea - 1 3/4 cups
- Sugar - 2 1/2 cups
- Cloves - 2 tsp
- Cinnamon - 4 tsp
- Tang - 22 oz jar
- Dry Lemonade Mix - 8 oz pkg

❖ Tools:

- Large Bowl
- Whisk (or Mom says "just a spoon" ;)
- 2-3 Quart Jars with lids

❖ Making Directions:

- Throw it all into the bowl and mix thoroughly (with either the whisk or spoon depending on whether you are listening to me or Mom).
- Distribute immediately into the jars evenly. Do it IMMEDIATELY or you will be forced to mix it again. This stuff settles out quickly.

❖ Mixing Directions:

- 1-3 tsp per 8 oz cup hot water (and maybe a jigger or two of Leiper's Fork Single Barrel).
- Note: Remember what I said above about this stuff settling? It will do it in the jar too, so shake that "blend" up before your grab your 1-3 tsp.

AUNT GAYLE'S FIRE AND ICE MARGARITA

(A MARGARITA WITHOUT THE ACID)

Aunt Gayle is Momma Dot's daughter and my husband's Aunt. She is a firecracker who has her momma's beautiful white hair. This woman can tear up a country dance floor and she helps keep the rowdy brood in line (unless we are all drinking her margaritas)! I recommend making a batch of her special brew and grabbing a dance partner for an absolutely amazing time!

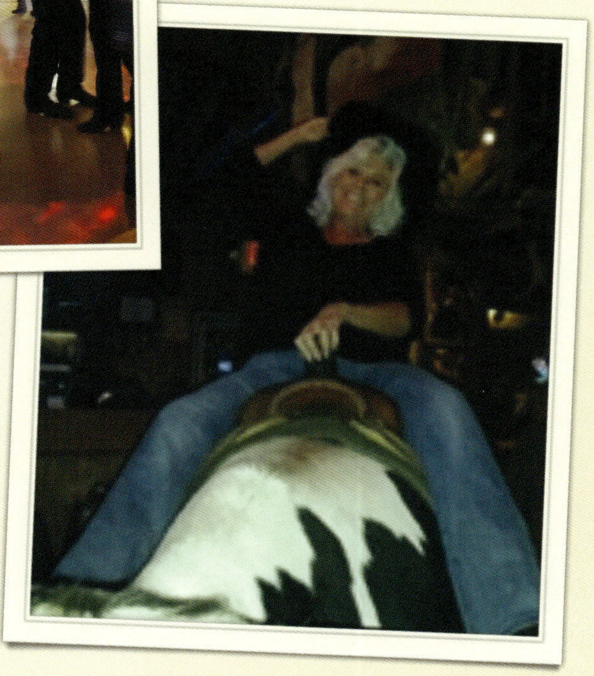

❖ Ingredients:

- Simply Lemonade - 1 bottle
  (or Simply Limeade, or Simply Lemonade Light)
- Poblano Pepper - 1
- Tequila

❖ Tools:

- Sharp Knife

❖ Directions:

- Cut poblano pepper into long, thin strips.
- Put the slices into the bottle of lemonade / limeade and return to the fridge.
- After a couple of days, you can mix this with your tequila, and you'll find the acid is gone from your margarita. Instead, it has a slight hot taste that is yummy! Fire and ice, so to speak.

THANKSGIVING DINNER MENU

(JUST A GUIDELINE TO GET YOU STARTED!)

Is there a more important meal than Thanksgiving dinner?? This is the one where we pull out all the stops, bring EVERYONE to the table, and serve up a little of everything. Your family's version will undoubtedly be different from ours, but maybe the list below will inspire you with some new ideas or challenge you to shake it up a little. This is the time to go overboard!

- Turkey & Cornbread Dressing (page 59)
- Ham
- Gravy
- Sweet Potato Casserole (page 74)
- Grean Peas / Beans
- Corn (try the version on page 60)
- Turnip Greens (page 75)
- Mac & Cheese (page 66) or Potato Salad
- Strawberry Salad
- Deviled Eggs (page 89)
- Waldorf Salad
- Stuffed Celery (stuff with cream cheese & chopped nuts)
- Confetti (Slaw) (page 129)
- Yeast Rolls (page 118)
- Cranberry Sauce (try the one on page 127)
- Side Condiments
- Iced Tea
- Coffee
- Wine
- Desserts (ask the kids to nominate their favorites!)

...and don't be afraid of making too much food. A fridge full of leftovers will give you something to be thankful for the next day!

HEINZ
TOMATO
KETCHUP

INDEX

NOTES

NOTES